H.M. Scudder

The Bazaar Book

Salzwasser

H.M. Scudder

The Bazaar Book

1. Auflage | ISBN: 978-3-84605-430-7

Erscheinungsort: Frankfurt, Deutschland

Erscheinungsjahr: 2020

Salzwasser Verlag GmbH

Reprint of the original, first published in 1869.

THE

BÀZAAR BOOK,

OR

VERNACULAR PREACHER'S COMPANION.

ORIGINALLY PREPARED

IN

TAMIL.

BY

REV. H. M. SCUDDER, D.D.,

AMERICAN ARCOT MISSION.

TRANSLATED

BY

REV. J. W. SCUDDER, M.D.

MADRAS:

PRINTED BY GRAVES, COOKSON AND CO.

1869.

PREFACE TO TAMIL EDITION.

WHEN the Rev. H. M. SCUDDER, D.D. had completed four numbers of his Bazaar Book, or Vernacular Preacher's Companion, he was prostrated by a severe illness and obliged to return to America. The remaining numbers, though written out, were left in an unfinished state. None of the explanations to the Tamil, Telugu and Sanscrit poetical quotations had been prepared. Dr. SCUDDER, on his departure, delivered over his manuscripts to the Publishing Committee of the American Arcot Mission, who have bestowed much time and labor in supplying what was needed to complete the work. The design of this treatise will be best explained in the author's own words :

"It contains addresses to heathen audiences, on the following subjects ;

I. THE GURU.	VIII. TRANSMIGRATION.
II. THE S'A'STRA.	IX. FATE.
III. SIN.	X. IDOLATRY SINFUL.
IV. MAN.	XI. IDOLATRY RUINOUS.
V. GOD.	XII. CASTE.
VI. EXPIATION.	XIII. BRAHMINISM.
VII. MANTRAS.	

"Each address is likewise intended to serve as a separate tract, complete in itself, and fit for independent distribution. Most of these addresses assume, as a starting point, some prominent falsity in Hinduism, which is exhibited and refuted as an introduction to the opposite truth; and such truth is, in each instance, displayed in connection with Him who said, 'I am the way, the truth, and the life.' Each address contains, woven into its texture, a few poetical quotations, selected with great care from Hindu works. These quotations are explained, word for word, in foot notes. Each address is also supplemented by an Appendix, in which are gathered such materials as one would not wish to find omitted, though they could not be allowed in the body of the address, without marring its unity, or too greatly increasing its bulk. Into these Appendices Telugu and Sanscrit, as well as Tamil citations are admitted. These too are analyzed and expounded, so that the reader shall have no need to apply to others for aid in their interpretation. While these addresses are constructed to stand as individual tracts, they constitute a series which, bound in a volume, shall furnish the Vernacular Preacher with many arguments and illustrations.

The author wishes it to be stated that in the numbers entitled CASTE and BRAHMINISM there is large indebtedness to the little Sanscrit treatise called VAJRA SUCHI.

A Supplementary Appendix, No. XIV, has been added in which are gathered those poetical quotations which could not be elsewhere classified, but which will prove useful to the Vernacular Preacher.

VELLORE, *May*, 1865.

NOTE TO TRANSLATORS.

THIS translation has been printed chiefly to facilitate the reproduction of the work in the various languages of India. Much of the popularity of the original depends upon the poetical quotations interspersed. Unless corresponding quotations are introduced from well-known writers, the effect will be disappointing. In most cases, these may be found by a careful search. There are some, however, by Tamil writers whom Dr. Caldwell supposes were more or less acquainted with Christianity. Although parallel quotations to such may not be available, a sufficient number may be obtained to give variety to the work.

The Addresses have been issued as Tracts by the Madras Tract Society.

MADRAS, 13*th September*, 1869.   J. MURDOCH.

CONTENTS.

THE BAZAAR BOOK.

ADDRESS No. I.

THE GURU.

ALL men everywhere agree in acknowledging and affirming their need of a Guru. That they are right in so doing may be established by various considerations. Some of these we shall try to set before you. We need a Guru;

FIRST.

BECAUSE OUR STAY IN THIS WORLD IS NOT PERMANENT.

Tiruvalluvar speaks thus on this subject:

CURAL, 34 : 6.

Literal Translation.

" The glory of this world may all be summed up in saying, that he who was born yesterday died to-day."

This is only too true. Our body is destined to death and decay. Not so, however, the soul, which resides within it. That is deathless, eternal. When the body dies, the soul will be forced to leave its tenement, and passing away, seek some other place beyond the bounds of this world.

Hear what Tayumanavar says of the body:

TAYUMANAVAR.

Literal Translation.

" Our body is the birthplace of foul insects and worms."

How true this is ! No sooner does the breath leave the body than those worms, increasing and multiplying by thousands, pervade all its members, roam at will through all its cavities, and fatten upon their spoil, until they have totally devoured it.

However much we may desire to remain in this world, we know that we cannot do so. As Pattanattu Pillai well expresses it :

PATTANATTU PILLAI.

Literal Translation.

" While we foolishly esteem this gross body to be ours ; the dog, the jackal and the vulture know that it is theirs. Therefore, O my Soul ! remembering that life is but vanity, and death an absolute certainty ; see that, even in your thoughts, you devise evil against no man."

Thus it is. Within the body, the insect and the worm await impatiently its dissolution. Without, the dog and the jackal, the vulture and the crow, looking with eager eyes, say, "The day this body dies will be to us a day of feasting and gluttony."

Dear Friends! Consider the well-known proverb, " As a bubble upon the stream, so fleeting, so transitory is the body."

Truly we have no stable abode in this world.* That our souls may attain to a good and permanent abode elsewhere, how necessary is it, that we should now seek and find a heavenly Guru ! Escape death we cannot. We are like one who, ignorant of the fording place, stands trembling upon the brink of a swelling river, which he must needs cross. That river is death. What alas ! shall we do ? We dare not leap into the roaring flood. But cross we must. Oh what need of a true Guru to show us the ford, to give us a helping hand, to support us when beyond our depth, and to bring us safely to the opposite shore ! Such a Guru each one of us must have, or perish.

We need a Guru ;

SECOND.

BECAUSE WE ARE DESTITUTE OF KNOWLEDGE.

What do we know about our own souls? What about the existence and nature of God ? What about

* See Appendix, page 15.

heaven? What about hell? Where is the man, whose knowledge can attain to these great mysteries? The more we reflect on them, the greater our confusion and bewilderment. Our heart, like a lampless house, is darkness itself. As in such a house hosts of bats congregate, and fly hither and thither, defiling and polluting it; so in our hearts great doubts and evil surmisings crowd innumerable, scattering bewilderment and pollution around. Can this lampless, lightless soul-house illuminate itself? Is it not from without that the light-giving torch must be sought for, and placed within it? The true Guru alone is an adequate lamp for our souls. Could such a one be found, he would shed light within us. He would teach us true wisdom. He would sever our doubts. He would chase away improper thoughts. He would give us a clear understanding. Such a Guru would be to us more precious than gold, dearer than shining rubies and pearls.

Pāmpātti Sittar speaks as follows :—

PAMPATTI SITTAR.

Literal Translation.

"There is a true creed, well fitted to instruct and guide into excellent paths those lying teachers who set forth a false religion. Strive, O my Soul! to reach the feet of the divine Guru who teaches what that true creed is."

We need a Guru;

THIRD.

BECAUSE WE ARE DESTITUTE OF MERIT.

When God, in the beginning, created the world and its inhabitants, they were good and perfect. Afterwards man, by violating God's law and falling into sin, ruined not only himself, but the world in which he dwelt. Thus sin overspread the whole earth. All order has become disorder. Look where we may, everything is disjointed and irregular. Sin has become earth's burden. All men, without exception, are sinners. Their own consciences abundantly testify to this fact. They themselves exhibit their conviction, that they are guilty. When we give expression to the thoughts of our hearts by writing them in visible letters upon paper, we show clearly to all, who read those letters, what our thoughts are. In like manner, all men, throughout the world, have given visible expression to the consciousness, that they are sinners. Do you ask me how? Behold the temples, which they have built; the tanks, which they have dug; the numberless places and rivers, which they have designated as sacred and .holy. All this they have done in order to remove their sins. It is true, that all these together cannot take away a single sin. But it is just as true, that men have thereby expressed the inmost thought of their hearts. The earth is their paper. The temple and the tank, the sacred shrine and the consecrated river are their letters. "We are sinners, self-convicted sinners," is what they have written. Wherever we go, this writing meets our eyes. This being so, who but a fool or a madman will venture to deny the existence of sin?

Brethren! Sinners we all are; but alas! not one of us has the power to remove his sin. If our sin is not taken away, hell must be our eternal abode. To whom shall we flee for succor? Oh if we might but find refuge with a true divine teacher! Then would our sins be taken away by the power of his merit. Such a teacher we all need. We need him to remove the load of our sins. and to cleanse our guilty, polluted souls.

. We need a Guru;

FOURTH.

BECAUSE WE ARE DESTITUTE OF TRUE JOY.

A soul without joy is like a field without a tank, a garden without a well. Such are we all. Many are our cares, abundant our anxieties and vexations, our sorrows and our troubles innumerable. Gather as much as we may of this world's wealth, the soul derives no true satisfaction from it. Enduring joy is a thing unborn. With bleeding hearts, we walk life's journey bewildered, sighing and wetting our path with our tears. The thought of the future fills us with fearful forebodings of evil. Oh! how greatly we need a heavenly, loving teacher to assuage our griefs, and heal our wounded hearts ; a Guru, who is able to comfort our souls, and to give our minds peace ; a divine Redeemer, who, rescuing us from the deep sea of affliction and planting our feet on the shore of happiness, shall protect us for evermore. Could we find such a one, we should rejoice as " the peacock, when it sees the approaching cloud." His favor would be to us as rain and dew to the parched and thirsty earth.

It is because such is our necessity, and because the divine Guru alone is able to meet and to minister to that necessity, that we hear all men in all countries crying out " We need a Guru." This is the world's lamentation.

Consider, now, what kind of a Guru he must be, who is qualified to meet the exigencies of our wretchedness. It is within the province of God alone to sustain and enlighten us, to rescue us from sin and fill us with joy. Hence it is plain, that God himself must come to be our Guru.

Ignorant of this great truth, millions follow after false Gurus. A most dangerous delusion this. To say that any mere man like ourselves is a divine teacher, and put our trust in him is a fatal mistake. There are thousands of bad men in the world, who, in order to deceive their fellows, give themselves out as Gurus. Such teach lying doctrines, and promulgate creeds both false and useless. Duping thousands, they rob them of countless money.* If you trust and adhere to such Gurus as these ; beyond a doubt, both you and they will fall together into one common, irretrievable ruin.

* See Appendix, page 15¼.

Listen to the story of the bear and the shepherd dying in a mutual embrace:

A bear with her cubs, having fallen into a flooded river, was borne rapidly down the stream. A simple shepherd spying the floating bear, mistook it for a sheep and eager, to catch the valuable prize, leaped into the swelling stream. The bear no sooner saw the swiming shepherd than, supposing him to be a raft and hoping by its means to gain the shore, it made directly for him. Thereupon the shepherd seizing the bear, and the bear laying hold of the shepherd; both of them, locked in a close embrace, went to the bottom never to rise again.

False Gurus, like that shepherd, seek only their own gain. Thousands, as foolish as the bear, suppose those false Gurus to be a saving raft. Such lying teachers, and all who are ignorant and besotted enough to trust in them, locked in a fatal embrace, must inevitably fall into hell, and share together a common and eternal ruin. Flee then all such deceiving Gurus. Venture not to approach them even for a moment. The God of Heaven must himself descend to earth and become our true Guru incarnate. Else our sin can never be removed.

But perhaps some of you will say, " Surely Vishnu is just such a divine Guru, adequate in all respects to our exigencies."· To this I reply, Listen to and ponder for a moment a few of the things which are related in your own Sastras concerning that same Vishnu. Those Sastras tell us, that Vishnu has ten incarnations. In his first incarnation, he was born as a fish ; in his second as a tortoise ; in his third as a swine ; in his fourth as a monster, half man, half lion. In his fifth incarnation, assuming the form of a dwarf Brahmin, named Vāmana, he cheated Mahābali, and tricked him out of his dominions. In his sixth, born as Parasurāma, he decapitated many kings. In his seventh, appearing as Rāma, he was robbed of his wife, and succeeded in kill-ing her ravisher only with the assistance of a monkey host. In his eighth, he became Krishna, and was notorious as a thief. In his ninth, born as Buddha, he taught the atheistical creed, which denies the existence of God and the human soul. In his tenth incarnation, which is still future, he will, it is predicted, flourish as a horse. Is it possible for any sane man to trust in a Guru, who is said to have taken such incarnations and committed such atrocities as these? Your Sastras declare, that Vishnu was born a fish and a swine, and that he wandered about as a thief and a debauchee. The bare acknowledgment of such a person as either God or Guru is in itself a heinous sin. This being so, it is clear as light, that Vishnu can never be a true Guru.

But others among you will perhaps ask, "Did not Siva, sitting as a Guru in the shade of the stone-banyan, teach divine truth? Why may we not accept him as a heavenly teacher?" To such we reply, Hear what is related about him in the Sivaite gospel, called the Skanda Purana.

Skanda Purana: Daksha Kandam: Uttara Padala.

Literal Translation.

"Siva the three-eyed one, having transformed Vishnu from his natural figure into a beautiful damsel, and having divested himself of his clothes, went, trident and mendicant's vessel in hand, accompanied by the metamorphosed Vishnu, into Tārugāvanam, celebrated among men as the sacred abode of the Rishis.

"Having entered the holy precincts, Siva, addressing Vishnu, spoke as follows, Go thou, approach all the places, where these congregated Rishis, thoughtless of me, have made their abode. Exercise all thy fascinations, and awaken within them libidinous desires. After thus compelling them to violate their vows of continency, return quickly to my side."

General Meaning.

Siva, having commanded Vishnu to assume the form of a lovely virgin, sent him to fascinate, bewilder and ruin the Rishis in Tārugāvanam. Besides this, Siva himself entered the same Tārugāvanam divested of his clothes and carrying his mendicant's vessel in his hand.

Such is the substance of the above verses. Following stanzas describe in detail the manner, in which Siva himself ravished the wives of the Rishis. But the story is too obscene to be quoted here.

According to your own Sastras then, this Siva, whom you extol as a divine Guru, not satisfied with inciting another to base and lascivious actions, himself lost all sense of decency, and roamed about naked, singing lewd songs and ravishing other men's wives. To what purpose is it then, that he taught, as you say, sitting under a stone-banyan tree, or for that matter under any other species of tree? Are we therefore to own him as a Guru? Are we to accept the instructions of a mouth, whence ribaldry and obscenity have proceeded, as the precepts of a divine teacher? Never. Siva can in nowise be acknowledged as the divine Guru.

Is there then no divine Guru incarnate, who is worthy of our confidence? There is. Jesus Christ is His name. He, and He alone, is the true, faithful, divine Guru incarnate, the Guru common to all mankind. His fulness compensates for all our defects. We are unstable, He is our firm foundation. We are ignorant, He is our wisdom. We are sinners, His holy deeds are our merit. We are sorrow-stricken, He is our joy. Let me speak of His attributes in detail.

FIRST.

This Guru is the Eternal God.

He is the Creator of heaven and earth, the Sovereign Ruler of all worlds. He is the Eternal, the First. Himself without beginning, He is before all other substances pre-existent; hence the Eternal. He is the

Creator of all substances, and therefore the beginning of all things. Possessor of these wonderful attributes, He left heaven, came down to earth, was born as a man, and thus became the God-Guru incarnate. Now this Jesus Christ, who is in one person the Eternal God and the good Guru, is to us, who are unstable and fleeting, a sure and firm foundation, whereon to build our trust and hope. Whoever believes in Him, though he die, shall by His grace reach heaven and live for ever. As the tree supports the vine which, clinging tendril by tendril, winds itself around its sturdy trunk; so Jesus Christ supports, preserves, and saves all those, who by a true faith lay hold upon him. Surely you will all consent, that the attainment of such a Guru would, to us poor unstable creatures, be of itself the wealth of heaven.

Hear Agastya's description of the true Guru.

AGASTYA.

Literal Translation.

" Approach, Oh my soul ! and worship the self-existent and eternal God, the Illuminator of the universe, who having in the twinkling of an eye created this vast world, and placed thereon perfect men, afterwards himself appeared upon it its incarnate Guru, lived in it as an ascetic without family relatives or pomp, practised religious austerities, established the school of his loving disciples, and finally returned to the eternal abodes of heaven."

Is there indeed such a Guru as this one of whom Agastya sings ? Yes there is one, and only one. Jesus Christ is that Guru. Sinful Soul ! Meditating on Him, pray in these words, " Oh Thou Eternal Guru ! Take possession of me, in such wise, that my soul, my body, and my all may be entirely and for ever thine."

SECOND.

THIS GURU IS THE ALL-WISE GOD.

The Christian Veda, which is the only true Sastra, is His Holy Word. In it He has taught us all that we need to know. By it He has communicated to us true knowledge about our souls, about God, about Heaven and about Hell. Christ's Holy Word is indeed the divine teaching of the true Guru.

Tāyumānavar speaks thus :—

TAYUMANAVAR.

Literal Translation.

" The word of the Guru is like a mountain way-mark. All other words are like a game of draughts played upon a checkerless board."

General Meaning.

As to a weary traveller, whose village is still in the invisible distance, the mountain, which towers by its side, stands evermore an immovable way-mark and guide ; so the word of the true Guru is to us an infallible leader, and will surely bring us to the invisible world of heaven. All other words are as profitless as would be an attempt to play a game of draughts upon an uncheckered board.

The Word of Jesus Christ alone is like the enduring and guiding mountain way-mark. Surely the finding and appropriation to our ignorant selves of such an All-wise Guru, is the highest good to which we can attain. Sinful Soul ! Looking to Him alone, pray saying : " Oh, Thou Lord of all Wisdom ! descend and dwell within me, that thus my heart may become thy holy temple."

THIRD.

THIS GURU IS THE INCARNATION OF ALL MERIT.

Having been born into this world, He remained in it thirty-three years. He dwelt in the midst of men, but He was a stranger to the wicked practices of sinners. In Him was never a spot, blemish or fault. Leading a most holy life, He illustrated by His actions the nature of true piety and virtue. Filled with pity for fallen men, He undertook the task of removing their sins. In behalf of men He obeyed and fulfilled all the laws of God, which they had broken and dishonored. In order to avert from men the punishment due to their violation of God's holy law, He suffered its penalty in their stead. For this purpose it was, that He was nailed to the cross, that He experienced inexpressible agonies, that He offered up his life as a sacrifice, died, and on the third day rose again from the dead. These deeds of His constitute the merit which saves lost sinners.* If we believe in Him, He will take away our sins, give His merits to us as our own, and granting us His Holy Spirit will cleanse and purify our souls.

But perhaps you will ask, "Why did Jesus suffer these terrible agonies? Had He not the power utterly to destroy the wicked men, who dared to nail Him to the cross, and take away His life?" Undoubtedly He had. He is the All-powerful Lord. Had He uttered one word of authority, it, like a thunderbolt falling on a palmyra, would have destroyed them in a twinkling. Why then did He yield Himself to such excruciating torments? Had He not done so, O People! our sin could never be removed. It was because He wished to abolish our sin, that, moved by tenderest love, He poured out His life in our behalf.

As Tiruvalluvar sings,

CURAL, 8 : 2.

Literal Translation.

"The loveless live only for themselves; but the loving deem not even their bones too costly a sacrifice for the good of others."

General Meaning.

Those, who are destitute of love, seek in every way to promote only their own interest and advancement; but those, who are possessors of true love, stand ready to give not only their wealth, but their very lives for the good of their fellow men.

* See Appendix, page 15¼.

Beloved! Consider for a moment the amazing nature of such love. Many are willing enough to be charitable. They will bestow upon others of their cattle, their land, their clothing, their food, their houses, their gold and the like. But these are, after all, only trifling gifts. It is no great thing to give in charity a cow or a piece of land, a cloth or a little rice, a house or a sum of money. But the gift of one's life; that may indeed be called great. Who is there, that is ready to bestow this? Offering one's life for one's dearest friend, though a thing almost unheard of, is possible. But who would give his life to save a malicious and ungrateful foe? Can such love be found any where in the wide world? No. Such love exists only in the heart of Jesus Christ, the divine Guru. All mankind are sinners and ungrateful rebels against God. Yet Jesus gave His life to save them from His wrath. Who shall undertake to tell the wonders of this love? It knows no superior, acknowledges no equal.*

Tāyumānavar addresses the Deity thus:

TAYUMANAVAR.

Literal Translation.

"I adore Thee, Oh Thou Fountain of all Bliss! who hast come incarnate to overflow my soul with love, and to rescue my precious life, my Lord and my God!"

These words can be said only of Jesus Christ. The Guru, the Lord, the God, the Fountain of Bliss, who has come to save us and to fill our souls with love, is He and He alone. There is none other in the broad universe.

Oh People! In Jesus Christ only is to be found merit adequate to scatter and drive away our sins. He is the virtue-distilling cloud, which must moisten and fertilize our barren souls. Can we contemplate His grace without a melting heart? When we think of His boundless love, is it not fit, that our stony breasts should dissolve like wax before the fire?

., We quote again from Tāyumānavar.

TAYUMANAVAR.

Literal Translation.

"That way is indeed the good way, which, taught by the grace of the Guru, causes our hearts to melt and leads us into heavenly bliss."

Brethren! Could we, who are utterly destitute of merit, only obtain the assistance of such a Guru as this Jesus Christ, who is Himself the very incarnation of all merit, what a boundless blessing it would prove to us! It would, as one of your proverbs says, be " like the falling of ripened fruit into milk." Sinful Soul! Look to Him. Beseech him thus, " Lord of my life, and hope! who, taking a body like mine, came, sought me out, and in infinite love laid down thy life in my behalf; redeem and save me, Oh Guru Immaculate!"

FOURTH.

THIS GURU IS THE PERSONIFICATION OF BENEVOLENCE
ND GRACE.

He mercifully bestows forgiveness of sin on those who cling to Him by faith. He comforts and guides them by His Spirit. He makes His love abound in their souls. He plants and cherishes in their hearts a sure hope of heavenly bliss. In this way, He removes from within them every vestige of grief and anxiety.

Enduring joy is the portion of all, whom He thus favors and blesses. However many may be their trials in this wicked world, they have but to think of their bliss-dispensing Saviour, they have but to look to the home He has prepared for them in the heavenly world, and immediately they receive strength sufficient to support patiently any and every sorrow. - The enduring thought of their heart is, " Oh Jesus Christ! My Guru! My God! My soul's Lover! My Sin-Destroyer! My sustaining, comforting Friend! Though all the world should desert me, Thou wilt never leave, Thou wilt never forsake me." Supported by this thought, they journey on with songs and rejoicings. Reading, believing, and meditating upon Christ's divine teachings, as recorded in the Holy Scriptures, they derive from them comfort and satisfaction so great, that, with bounding hearts and beaming countenances, they tread the path He has marked out for them. His precious Word flows evermore like a blissful river through their souls. To what shall we liken that word? If we liken it to honey, honey will lose its sweetness. If we compare it to gold, gold can no longer be esteemed precious. If to jewels and gems, the pearl and the diamond must cease their corruscations. The heart, that hears and accepts Christ's Word, blooms expanding like the lotus that sees the rising Sun. Embrace Him, Oh Sinful Soul! Extol Him in these words, "Fountain of all Light and Joy! More precious art Thou than jewels and gold; dearer than parents, wife and offspring; Life of my life! Shoreless Ocean of Eternal Bliss!"

Oh People! It is because you know not this true Guru, that you worship stocks and stones.

Witness what Sangarāsāriar says :—

SANGARASARIAR.

Literal Translation.

"The degraded of the earth, ignorant of the divine Guru, and giving heed to the treacherous teachings of false Gurus, adore and worship stones believing them to be gods. A moment's reflection will suffice to convince, that, by accepting the word of these lying Gurus, Hell and not Heaven must be our lot. Ancient sages tell us, that those, who learn to know the true Guru, immediately attain to heavenly bliss."

Brethren! Cast away your idols of wood and stone. Relinquish your vain and fruitless ceremonies. Come to the Lord Jesus Christ, the eternal, omniscient, merit-abounding, gracious Guru. If you approach Him not, you will assuredly fall into the fire of Hell. If you reach His feet, He will at once remove the guilt of your sins, and the pollution of your souls. Through Him you will obtain purity of heart and heavenly felicity.

The Nāladiār speaks as follows:—

NALADIAR, 18 : 5.

Literal Translation.

"The slush of a village drain, if it falls into a flowing river, changes its very name and is called pure; so the base, if they but associate with nobles, stand eminent as a towering mountain."

General Meaning.

The polluted water of a village drain, if it discharges into a large river, loses its filth and becomes pure. Its very name is changed, and men henceforth call it clean. So vile persons, if they associate with the good, themselves becoming good, stand eminent and firm as a mountain.

You well know the proverb also which says: "Even the cord which binds flowers together becomes fragrant."

Beloved! Mankind are all bad; Jesus Christ alone is good. If we believe in Him, we shall obtain pardon, holiness, and eternal glory.

APPENDIX to No. I.

ILLUSTRATIONS AND EXAMPLES.

(1.) Our stay in this world is not permanent.

VEMANAR.

Literal Translation.

"Oh Vēmanar! However long one lives in this world, however persistently he studies, or however pre-eminently he shines; within a few short days he must die, and then all his learning will become but dust."

PATTANATTU PILLAI.
Literal Translation.

"The fire, the worm, the earth, the vulture, the jackal and the dog claim my body as their own, saying, 'This is ours to devour.' Most lovingly have I cherished this fleeting body. But what, alas! have I profited thereby?"

(2.) Gurus enough there are, who rob us of our money. What we need is a true sorrow-dispelling Guru.

SANSCRIT SLOKA.
Literal Translation.

"Numberless, Oh my Soul! are the gurus, who seize and carry off the money of their disciples. But where, alas! shall we seek for the true Guru, who shall remove and destroy our sorrows and our woes?"

(3.) Heaven is the result not of our own, but of the Guru's good deeds.

NISHTANUPUTI, 3RD STANZA.
Literal Translation.

"Ancient sages tell us, that Heaven can never be obtained by mastering the three degrees in the Saiva system, named Saritai, Kiriyai and Yogam. But it is undeniable that supreme felicity is procured by the matchless truths taught by the divine Guru."

Jesus Christ alone is the teacher of those matchless truths. None but He has either the authority, or the power, to announce them to men. The sum of His gracious words is this; "Oh Sinner! I have borne your sins on the cross. Trust me, love me, and walk in the way, which I point out to you, and I will assuredly give you Heaven."

(4.) A free gift is the best of all gifts.

CURAL 11: 1.
Literal Translation.

"The gift of earth and heaven combined is not to be compared to a benefit conferred where none had been previously received."

Beloved! Is there any one, think you, that can confer a benefit upon Jesus Christ, the true God and divine Guru? The three worlds together cannot furnish such a person. Consider now, that we have rebelled against this same true God and divine Guru. And yet, He gave His very life to save us sinners and rebels from Hell. Though one should bestow upon us earth and heaven, even that could not for a moment be compared to the boundless gift, which He has conferred. Lay then your hearts, Oh People ! as a willing offering at the feet of this most gracious divine Guru, and love Him in return for His free and unbounded love to you !

SCRIPTURE PROOFS.

(1.) Jesus Christ, the Redeemer of the world, is the Creator and Preserver of all things :
Colossians 1. 16, 17.

(2.) He is God Incarnate :
Romans 9. 5 ; 1 Timothy 3. 16 ; 1 John 5. 20.

(3.) He died and rose to save sinners :
Romans 5. 6 to 8 ; Romans 8. 34 ; 1 Peter 2. 24.

(4.) He is the Eternal God-Guru :
Isaiah 6. 6 ; Rev. 22. 13 ; Hebrews 13. 8.

(5.) He is the All-wise Divine Guru :
Colossians 2. 3 ; Colossians 2. 9 ; John 2. 24, 25.

(6.) He is the incarnation of all merit :
Hebrews 7. 26 ; 1 Peter 3. 18 ; 1 John 3. 5 ;
Jeremiah 23. 6.

(7.) He is the personification of all benevolence and grace :
Matthew 11. 28 ; John 10. 11 ; John 6. 36.
Galatians 2. 20 : Malachi 4. 2 ; Revelations 5. 11, 14.

(8.) Besides Him, there is no other Saviour :
Acts 4. 12 ; Hebrews 4. 14.

ADDRESS No. II.

THE SASTRA.

ALL mankind have left the true God, and become wanderers in the ways of sin. Enveloped by the darkness of ignorance, they roam hither and thither, perplexed, bewildered and dismayed. The truth of this none will venture to deny.

This being so, it is plain, that men need the torch of a true Sastra to dispel the darkness, show them the way, and bring them back to God.*

Tāyumānavar, one of your poets, says,

Literal Translation.

" Oh God ! Is there never an excellent lamp of wisdom whereby thou canst dispel this dense darkness (of ignorance) in which I am so closely enveloped, that I cannot discern a single thing ?"

General Meaning.

I am in darkness so thick that I can perceive nothing. Oh God ! Is there no lamp of wisdom to dispel this terrible night of ignorance ? That such a lamp of wisdom is necessary, all of us will readily admit. Could we but obtain the true Sastra, which God has graciously given, that would indeed prove to be the lamp we all need.

If we search throughout the world, we find that Sastras abound in it. But the question is, " Are they all true, and as such fit to be accepted and relied on ?" Assuredly all these, who without inquiry as to their truth or falsity, pronounce any and all Sastras to be good, are treading upon dangerous ground. You have heard the proverb which says that, " He who neither investigates nor considers deserves to perish." We find

---

* That a Sastra is necessary, see Sloka on page 28 of the Appendix.

in the world money current, and money uncurrent. Who is so foolish as to accept both as equally valuable? To examine well, and accept only the good, is the part of the wise.

In the Nāladiār we find the following :

"Countless is the number of Sastras, but few are the days of those who study them, exposed to a thousand fatalities. Therefore like the Swan, which separating the milk from the water with which it is mingled drinks only the former ; let the wise carefully discriminating reject worthless Sastras, and study only those which are valuable."

Now, if we thus carefully discriminate, we shall soon arrive at the conclusion, that there is and can be only one true Sastra in the world. God who created all men everywhere is Himself one. Can we at all suppose, that He would give men numberless Sastras, each one of which is at variance with all the others? Certainly not. As He has created only one Sun to shed a common light upon all men in all lands, we may reasonably conclude that in like manner He would give only one Sastra common to all. It is our part to find out which, among the many Sastras, that one true Sastra is. Let us then inquire a little concerning it.

Will you assert that the four Vedas, written in the Sanscrit language, constitute that true Sastra? Assert it as much as you will, your assertion will never hold good.

Look for a moment at the various and contradictory statements, which your books make about these four Vedas.

In certain of your treatises, it is affirmed, that the four Vedas were never made, but are themselves Eternal.* In others it is declared, that the same four Vedas were born from the four faces of Brahma.† Now it is evident enough, that if the latter statement is true, the former must be false. If born from Brahma's face, they are certainly not Eternal.

* & † For examples see Slokas, &c., on page   of the Appendix.

Again : The Bhagavata, on the one hand, tells us, that in the beginning there was only one Veda; but that subsequently it was made into three by king Purúvaran in Trētāyuga, the second or silver age.* The Vishnu Purana on the other hand declares, that Vishnu, becoming incarnate as Veda Vyasa, divided the one original Veda into four in the Dvāpara Yuga, or third age of the world.† At complete variance with both the above statements, we are informed in the last chapter of the Brahma Purana, that Siva, having created Brahma, communicated the Vedas to him.‡

Nor have we done yet. Listen further. In the book called Harivamsa, we are taught, that Brahma having constructed the Gāyatri Mantra, caused the four Vedas to proceed out of it.§ But the Mānava Dharma Sastra teaches us positively, that Brahma milked the Rig Veda from Agni or Fire, the Yajur Veda from Vayu or Wind, and the Sama Veda from the Sun.‖ Now, besides the fact that these two accounts are subversive the one of the other; is it not plain that the latter, which affirms, that the Vedas were milked out of Fire, Wind and Sun is far better fitted to provoke our laughter than our faith ?

Oh People! Which of all the many stories told in your books about the Vedas are we to believe ? Which of these numerous contradictory statements are we to accept as right ? One work tells us, that the Vedas are without beginning and eternal. Another says Not so, they were born from the four faces of Brahma. A third, pronouncing both the above statements wrong, affirms that the Veda, originally but one, was divided into three Vedas by a certain king. All stuff and nonsense, screams a fourth, it was no king, but Vishnu himself who made the one Veda three. As mistaken as the rest, shrieks a fifth; for it was Siva, who having created

* & † & ‡ For these statements, see Slokas, &c., on page　　　of the Appendix.

§ & ‖ For these statements, see Slokas, &c., on page　　　of the Appendix.

Brahma communicated to him the Vedas. Every one of you wrong, roars a sixth, for is it not well ascertained, that Brahma milked the Vedas out, just as a milkman does a cow? Now these various statements are all contained in your own books. What a bewildering medley! Assuredly the origin of your four Vedas is involved in inextricable doubts and hopeless confusion.

Again, still another of your Sastras tells us that the four Vedas proceeded originally out of Brahma's mouth. But do you not all well know, that this same Brahma is without a single worshipper, because he told a lie? It does not satisfactorily appear how a Veda, emanating from the mouth of a liar, can be true.

Observe yet another thing. The rule is laid down in your Sastras, that the Vedas appertain only to Bramins and others, who like them are invested with the sacred cord;* but that women and Sudras are in no case to read or even hear them read.† How is this? Can we suppose that God, in giving a Veda, would deny it to Sudras, and bestow it only upon those who wear a cord? Is it to these alone that he gives his rain, his wind, and his sun-shine?

Furthermore, these four Vedas are written in Sanscrit, a language utterly unknown and unintelligible to ordinary people. They are rendered still more difficult by numberless transmutations, augmentations, and elisions. They have been purposely made abstruse and obscure. Not one in a thousand, even among Bramins, can read and explain them. Such Vedas are utterly useless to the world of mankind. Hence we cannot allow for a moment that these four Vedas have God for their author. Far from being divinely revealed, they are evidently the productions of fraudulent and tricky Bramins.

But perhaps some of you will say, "It may be true, that the four Vedas are practically useless. But surely there are the two Itihasas, viz., the Maha Bharata and the Ramayana, and the eighteen Puranas which toge-

---

* & † For these rules, see Slokas on page   of the Appendix.

ther constitute the fifth Veda.* These we hold to be
the true divine Sastra." To such we reply, Listen a
moment, and you will see that you are wrong.

Those Itihasas and Puranas are full of errors and false
statements about the very Earth on which we dwell.
We give only an example or two here. "One grain of
boiled rice suffices to test a potful."

Nallā Pillai Bārata. A'ti Paruvam : Salarkāra Sarukam :—

Literal Translation.

" The thousand-headed Ati Séshan who bestows the excellence, which is a jewel in his faultless crown, in virtue of the
gift bestowed upon him by the fragrant lotus-dwellingBrahma
for penance performed, placing all the worlds upon his in-
comparably majestic head, dwelt in Nāgalōga."

General Meaning.

The thousand-headed serpent named A'tiséshan, in
virtue of the gift bestowed on him by Brahma, supports
on his head the burden of all the worlds.

Oh People ! Has any one ever really seen or heard of
such a thing as a snake with a thousand heads ? Besides, do we not see with our own eyes, that the Sun
hangs entirely unsupported in the sky ? The earth
hangs in precisely the same way.

It is Almighty God, who by his power sustains the
earth in the firmament. Who then can avoid laughing,
when he is told that the same earth rocks upon the head
of a snake ?

As if this gigantic fabrication were not enough, hear
another bare-faced falsehood which your Purāna, without either fear or shame, tells about this earth.

Skanda Purāna.   Asura Kāndam.   Andakōsappadalam :†

Literal Translation.

" In this broad world, the seven seas, viz., the sea of salt
water, of milk, of buttermilk, of ghee, of sugarcane juice,

---

* See Sloka on page   of the Appendix.
† See what is said in Sanscrit about the seven seas on page   of
the Appendix.

of spirituous liquor, and of clear water, severally touch upon and surround each of its seven great continents. Beyond these seas, the mountain Sakvaravālam encompasses the entire golden earth."

General Meaning.

The wide world is made up of seven islands or continents. Seven seas surround these seven continents. Their names are as follows; the sea of salt water, the sea of milk, the sea of buttermilk, the sea of ghee, the sea of sugarcane juice, the sea of spirituous liquor, and the sea of clear water. Beyond these seas stands the mountain Sakvaravālam, encompassing the whole.

Oh People! Besides the one great salt sea, there is no other on this earth. All this talk about a sea of milk, and a sea of spirituous liquors, and a sea of ghee, and various other seas, is like the sportive babbling of little children.

This is by no means the end of the false statements, which your Itihasas and Puranas tell about this world. There are many more of the same sort. We quote another in this place.

Skanda Purāna. Asura Kāndam. Andakōsappadalam :

Literal Translation.

"Mount Meru, which stands in the midst of the central Swerga-like continent of Jambu, is in form like the seed-vessel of the red lotus. Its height is 84,000 yojanas, (equal to 1,092,000 miles.) It extends to a depth of 16,000 yojanas (equal to 208,000 miles) below the surface of the earth. The breadth of its top is 32,000 yojanas (equal to 416,000 miles.) The circumference of its base near the earth is half of the last mentioned number, (that is 16,000 yojanas, (equal to 208,000 miles.) It terminates in three most beautiful peaks, the middle one of which is crowned with many smaller peaks."

General Meaning.

A prodigious mountain, called Mahá Meru, stands on the centre of the earth. This mountain towers up in the sky to the height of 1,092,000 miles. It extends

below the earth's surface to a depth of 208,000 miles.
Its top is 416,000 miles broad, and the circumference of
its base measures 208,000 miles.

Hear now what is said further about this amazing
mountain in the Skanda Purāna :—

Literal Translation.

" On the South side of mount Meru stands a fragrant
Nāval or Jambu tree. From this tree it is, that the entire
country ruled over by king Bharata derives its name of Na-
valan Dwipa or Jambu Dwipa. The juice of the luscious
fruit of this tree, forms a vast river called Sāmpunata, which,
after encircling the wide base of mount Meru, flows towards the North. All who drink of its waters have their
bodies turned into gold, and live there 13,000 years."

General Meaning.

On the south side of Maha Meru stands a Naval tree.
The juice of the fruit hanging on its boughs, flowing
like a river around the base of the mountain, runs toward the north. All who drink of this river become
endowed with forms of gold, and have their lives prolonged to a period of 13,000 years.

Oh People! Is there anywhere on this wide earth a
mountain 1,092,000 miles high ? Is there anywhere a
tree so immense, that the juice of its fruit runs like a
river ? Where will you find the men who, having drunk
of that juice, are living out their 13,000 years, endowed
with golden bodies ? If such life-giving juice really
exists in any place, would not the whole world run as
one man, and drink of it ? But the entire story is nothing else than a prodigious fable. White men have
thoroughly explored every spot on the surface of this
earth. There is no such mountain. There is no such
tree. There is no such juice. There is no such golden
form. There is no such longevity.

Now mark well the three statements which we have
quoted above, viz., that there is a snake-world beneath
this earth; that seven oceans swell within its bowels,
and that Mount Meru towers above its surface. When
we discover in your Itihāsa Puranas such prodigious

falsehoods as these about the lower, central, and upper parts of the earth; does it not plainly appear, that piling lie upon lie was a mere pastime to the authors of those works?

After your Itihāsa Puranas have given us such false and deceptive statements regarding this world, which we see with our eyes, how can we possibly accept the still more absurd statements, which those same Puranas make about unseen worlds and about the invisible God? Unquestionably they are to be rejected as equally false and deceptive.

But some of you will ask; "Even if the Vedas, and the Itihāsas and the Puranas are to be rejected as false, there still remain the Agamas, the Siddhantas and the Vedantas. Why may we not regard these as a true, divine Sastra?" To this we reply as follows:

In a true divine Sastra graciously bestowed by God there must be clearly and definitely set forth one and only one way to Heaven, which shall be equally suited to all men of every clime. But in the works you have just named, we discover no such heavenly way. The path by which men may obtain the removal of their sins, and attain eternal bliss is nowhere to be found in any of them. The ways, which are pointed out in these works as conducive to those ends are indeed numerous. But they are as useless as they are contradictory. They are like the many devious and aimless paths trodden out by wild beasts wandering hither and thither in a great uninhabited waste. They lead to no town. If any one attempt to follow them, he will, instead of reaching a village, become more and more involved in difficulty, until thoroughly staggered and bewildered, he will fall into some pit and there die. Your religious works are just like such a vast waste. All who venture to walk in the paths they indicate will fall into hell, and never see the goodly land of heaven. How can we suppose even for a moment, that books which thus bewilder and destroy men are the true divine Sastra?

If after what has been said, further reasons are neces-sary to prove that your Sastras, far from being divinely bestowed, are but the false productions of deceitful de-signing men, they shall not be wanting.   Listen.

There is but one God, the Ruler of all worlds.   But your Sastras, failing to make Him known, direct you to worship 330,000,000 of gods.   Is not the statement, that there are 330,000,000 gods, itself composed of 330,000,000 lies ?

Again, your Sastras, ignorant of the perfectly holy na-ture of the one God, have blasphemously dared to attri-bute sin to Him.   Not satisfied with declaring that there are innumerable gods, they tell us, that those gods com-ing into this world committed all sorts of wickedness. They relate, that one of those gods, named Brahma, told a lie ; that another of those gods, called Vishnu, stole butter, and that a third, styled Siva, ravished the wives of the Rishis.   Inventing such vile stories as these, they have shut out from the people of this land all know-ledge of the true nature of God, and have involved them in bewildering errors.   God is not such an one as they declare him to be.   We must inevitably decide, that Sastras, which so represent God, are nothing more nor less than a pack of ribald fables.

Besides this, there are in your Sastras numberless obscene stories, which are well calculated to arouse the vilest passions, to utterly ruin the mind, and to drag men into adultery, fornication, and all other kinds of wickedness.   Such disgusting stories abound in the Bharata, the Bhagavata, and in the Skanda Purāna. The bare mention of them is an impropriety, and we omit them here for very shame.   What tongue will venture the assertion, that a Sastra containing obscene stories is the true, divine, God-given Sastra ?

Hear one more reason general and comprehensive.

You affirm, that the four Vedas, the eighteen Puranas, the twenty-eight Agamas, the sixty-four Kalaignanas, the Menu Vigngana, the various Vedantas and the Siddhantas are all true, divinely-inspired Sastras.   If so, it is a duty to read, ponder, and master the whole of them. But no one's life is long enough for the task. Moreover, these Sastras are all composed in difficult verses, so that they may be of no avail to ordinary men. It is immensely hard to read, and still more difficult to ascertain their meaning. Would a God-given Sastra be like these? Would God not rather bestow one easily intelligible to all? And would He not condense it within such limits, that the reading of it should not be an impossibility?

Oh People! Reject these worthless Sastras, which, as we have shewn you, are the compositions of deceivers. Acknowledge as true the following statement made concerning them by your own poet Saṅgarāsāriar :—

" All the Sastras composed by the ancient sages of this world have failed to give any true account of the Eternal God. More than this, those sages having divided those Sastras into numberless contradictory fragments, and having lied like devils, have themselves all been swallowed up in the terrible pit of hell."

Brethren! There is a true Sastra. Its substance is veracious and divine. In it there is neither falsehood, nor alloy. It reveals sound doctrine and true wisdom. It drives away the clouds of ignorance, as the wind does the clouds of the sky.

That true Sastra is none other than the Christian Veda.

This Christian Veda is within such a compass, that all can easily read it through. Its nature is such, that it can be readily translated and published in every language of every country in the world. It is written in prose so simple, that all persons can read it without difficulty.

Furthermore, it is perfectly plain and intelligible. Any one can read it, any one can understand it, any one can meditate on it. Even those, who are not readers, may by the ear easily apprehend its truths, and discover the good way of salvation.

This true Sastra teaches us, that there is one only
true God, and reveals his nature to us.   If we read this
sacred Veda with an humble faith, we can arrive at a
true knowledge of God and of his holy nature as easily
as a man, looking at himself in a mirror, can discern
the features of his face.

Obscene stories, conducive to lust and lasciviousness,
are nowhere to be found in this Christian Veda.   There
is not in it one single thing that can injure the mind.
On the contrary, it is filled to overflowing with instruction calculated to make men think of their sins, mourn
over them, relinquish them, and return with loving confidence to God.

Furthermore, this Sastra points out the way by which
men may get rid of their sins, and attain to the felicity
of heaven.   Listen attentively, while we enlarge a little
upon this point.

We have all broken the laws of God and sinned
grievously against him. We are utterly destitute of
all power to remove our sins, or to escape from hell,
or to gain heaven.   To save us, who are thus complete-
ly ruined and helpless, Jesus Christ became incarnate
in this world.   This Jesus Christ is the Lord of lords.
Leaving heaven, he descended to this earth and was
born as a man.   He lived upon it thirty-three years.
He shone pre-eminent as the divine God-Guru.   He
sent forth his grace like sunlight.   He also removed our
sins.   Were a mountain to be plucked up, and placed
upon your heads, could you sustain its weight ? You
could not. It would crush and destroy you. Just so your
sin is sure to crush you down into hell, and destroy you
with an everlasting destruction.   Jesus Christ came for
the very purpose of himself bearing and removing our
sins, which are heavier than many mountains together.
That we might not suffer the punishment of hell, he was
punished in our stead on this earth.   It was for this,
that he was nailed to the cross. He gave his own life
to redeem the life of man. He arose again from the
dead, and ascended back to heaven. He is the sinless

Holy One. All he did upon earth was meritorious. If we believe on him, the punishment due to us will be averted by his sufferings, and by the righteousness he wrought out our sin will be removed, and we will gain heaven. This is the way. There is no other.

Observe, that the way taught in this true Sastra is but one. That way is simply to renounce all sin, believe in Jesus Christ and lovingly obey him. All who enter upon and walk in this way will, through Jesus Christ, gain the eternal bliss of heaven. All who do not enter upon this way will fall into eternal hell.

Thus, this true Sastra points out anew the path to us, who have lost our way; shines with heavenly radiance upon us who are immersed in darkness; rescues us from the howling wilderness in which we have become inextricably involved; gives a helping hand to us, who are bereft of all strength, and brings us, wandering ungrateful rebels, back to God. This is just such a Sastra as we all need. The Christian Veda is the one only true Sastra, which God has graciously bestowed upon man.

Beloved! A false Sastra is like poison. He who takes it cannot live. Your Sastras being such, renounce them at once. But Christ's True Veda is like heavenly nectar. His word is the elixir of eternal life. He who takes it will live for ever in heaven. If you do not accept it, you are your own destroyers.

Tiruvalluvar tells us that,[*]

" The stupid soul, which rejects the precious Veda, does itself incalculable injury."

Do not obstinately argue saying, " Our Sastras were born with us. How then can we renounce them ?"

There is an old song of yours which is as follows :

" Think not that those who were born with you are therefore true relatives. The disease, that is born with us, kills us ; the medicine, which is found on some far off mountain, though it was not born with us, cures our natal disease. There are those in the world, who are like that medicine."

* Cural, Chap. 85, 7.

The thought in this verse is beautiful and true. The disease, born with us, kills us; the medicine not born with us, but produced on some distant mountain, cures our natal disease.

The disease born with you is your Sastra. The Christian Veda, which has now come to you from a far off land, is the medicine which is fitted to cure that disease.

By degrees this Christian Veda will get firm hold in this country of yours. Men will see its excellence and exult in it. Then all false Sastras will flee away. Grass will grow in their receding tracks, and not one man will be found to follow after them.

Some persons call the *ignis fatuus*, which appears at night in waste places, a fiery-mouthed devil. It is not a devil. It is merely a peculiar kind of gas, which is generated in swamps, and at night has the appearance of fire. It is generally seen playing and dancing over places, where pits filled with mud and deep mire abound. Sometimes persons, lost in such places, seeing this false flame and supposing it to be a village lamp, follow it about, until bewildered they fall into the pits, sink into the mire and perish. In like manner, a false Sastra shewing a false light, inveigles men into the pit of hell. The true Sastra, on the contrary, is like a cottage lamp. When one, who has lost his way, sees such a light; he is not deceived. Fixing his eyes upon it as a guide, he soon reaches the house, and relieved of all trouble and anxiety, enjoys the comforts of his home. So he who, procuring the Christian Veda, reads it with a believing heart, and follows its teachings will assuredly reach heaven, the home of eternal bliss, and for ever enjoy its incalculable felicity.

APPENDIX TO No. II.

EXAMPLES AND ILLUSTRATIONS.

(1.) **Men need a Sastra.**

HITOPADESA.

Translation.

" He is indeed a blind man, who is without the Sastra

which severs many doubts, reveals what is invisible, and is itself an eye to all who possess it."

(2.) Example affirming, that the four Vedas of the Hindus were not made; but are themselves eternal.

VEDANTA SIDDHANTA SAMAVEDA: VASTU NISCHAYA.

Translation.

" The four Vedas are from eternity. The excellent substance of those Vedas is true substance. All who acquire a clear knowledge of that substance are thereby freed from every distress, and having entered into a state of enduring and unchangeable certainty, will for ever flourish in the midst of heavenly felicity."

(3.) Example affirming that the four Vedas of the Hindus sprung from the four faces of Brahma.

B'HAGAVATA: 3RD SKANDHA, 12TH AD'HYAYA.

Translation.

" The Vedas were produced by Brahma the four-faced, while in contemplation as to the plan by which he might again create the hosts of worlds in the same manner as at first. He caused the four Vedas named the Rig, the Yajur, the Sama, and the Atharvana to spring in order from his four faces, beginning with his East face. He also created Muntras, Sacrifice, Melody and Expiation."

(4.) Example affirming that in the beginning the Veda was but one, and that subsequently it was divided into three by king Purūvaran.

B'HAGAVATA: 9TH SKANDHA, 14TH AD'HYAYA.

Translation.

" Oh king! In the beginning, the Veda was but one. The all-comprehensive Pranava Mantra* was that Veda. The three Vedas were issued by Purūvaran at the opening of the Trētāyuga."

(5.) Example affirming that Vishnu, taking the form of Veda Vyasa, divided the one original Veda into four in the Dvāpara Yuga.

* The Pranava Mantra is the mystic Om.

VISHNU PURANA.

Literal Translation.

" Vishnu, on several occasions, taking the form of Veda Vyasa divided the one Veda into four parts, and amplified it into a hundred subdivisions."

General Meaning.

Vishnu, assuming the form of Veda Vyasa divided the Veda, which was one, into four Vedas, and amplified it by numerous sub-divisions.

(6.) Example affirming, that Siva created Brahma, and communicated the Vedas to him.

BRAHMOTTARA KANDAM:

Descriptive of the great Rudra's glory.

Literal Translation.

" Wherefore be not troubled (oh king!) Hear (what is told). Siva the formless, the immaculate, the effulgent, created Brahma by the Raja-guna, which is one among the three gunas, (viz., Satva, Raja and Tama) that he assumed of his own free will, and at the same moment graciously conferred upon him all the Vedas."

General Meaning.

Siva having created Brahma by Raja-guna, which is one of the three gunas he of his free will assumed, taught him at the same time all the Vedas and Sastras.

(7.) Example affirming that Brahma, having made the Gayatri Mantra, caused the four Vedas to proceed out of it.

HARIVAMSA.

Literal Translation.

" Then he created the Gayatri, which, composed of three metrical feet, is the mother of Vedas. He also made the four Vedas, which were born from the Gayatri."

General Meaning.

Brahma created the Gayatri Mantra, which is the mother of Vedas, and has three metrical feet. From that Gayatri, he caused the four Vedas to spring.

In direct contradiction to this last example, it is affirmed in the Mānava-Dharmma Sastra, that Brahma milked the Gayatri Mantra out of the three Vedas.

MANAVA DHARMMA SASTRA. 2ND AD'HYAYA, 77TH SLOKA.

Translation.

" Brahma milked out from the three Vedas, in order, the three feet of the Gayatri Mantra, which begins with the word Tat."

(8) Example affirming that Brahma milked the Vedas from Fire, Wind, and Sun.

MANAVA DHARMMA SASTRA. 1ST AD'HYAYA, 23RD SLOKA.

Literal Translation.

" In order to the accomplishment of Sacrifice, he (Brahma) milked from Fire, the Wind and the Sun the three eternal Vedas, named the Rig, the Yajur, and the Sama."

General Meaning.

In order that sacrifices might be successfully offered, Brahma milked the Rig Veda from Fire, the Yajur Veda from Wind, and the Sama Veda from the Sun.

(9) It is laid down as a rule in the work called the Vedārtha Prakasá that the Vedas are only for Brahmans and others who are invested with the sacred cord.

Literal Translation.

" Wherefore the connexion of the Veda is only with the three castes (viz., Brahman, Kshattriya, and Vaisaya) who wear the sacred cord."

General Meaning.

The Veda is for the three castes, who are invested with the sacred cord, viz., Brahmans, Kshattriyas and Vaisayas ; and is not intended for any others.

(10) Example affirming that women and Sudras may not even hear the Vedas.

Literal Translation.

" The threefold Veda is not a thing (intended) for the ears of women, of Sudras, or of the twice-born who have lost their caste."

General Meaning.

Women and Sudras, and such of the twice-born as have lost caste, are not permitted even to hear the three Vedas, named Rig, Yajur, and Sama.

(11.) Example affirming that the Itihasas and Puranas were created a fifth Veda.

B'HAGAVATA : 3RD SKANDHA, 12TH AD'HYAYA.

Literal Translation.

" The all-seeing Isvara, from out of all his faces, created the Itihasa-Puranas as the fifth Veda."

(12.) Example affirming that there are seven seas.

Literal Translation.

" Seven encircling seas were created, whose contents are (in order) salt water, sugarcane juice, spirituous liquor, ghee, milk, buttermilk and clear water."

Some further examples showing that the Sastras of the Hindus are false.

Example affirming that the Earth is supported by eight elephants.

B'HAGAVATA : NARASINGHA PATALA.

Literal Translation.

" At the call of the deceitful Asuras, the eight elephants who support the cardinal points (of the earth) and who are named Anjana, Kumuda, Vamana, Jaravata, the matchless Pun'dareeka, the renowned mountain-like Pushpadanta, Suprateepa shining as truth, and Sarvvabhouma, who crushes his affrighted foes, came like eight mountains trembling."

General Meaning.

At the summons of the Asuras, the eight elephants who support the earth came trembling. Their names are as follows: Anjana, Kumuda, Vamana, Jarāvata, Pun'dareeka, Pushpadanta, Suprateepa and Sarvvabhouma.

Remarks.

Oh People! In a former quotation it was affirmed, that a thousand-headed snake supports the earth on his crest. The verse just quoted would seem to indicate, that eight elephants help the afore-mentioned snake, by giving their backs also to sustain the burden. The former story is a lie; the latter story is a lie. Why do you believe in, and adhere to your Sastras, which tell such falsehoods as these?

Example affirming that, Brahma, being born inside of an egg, afterwards broke the egg into two parts, and out of those parts framed the heaven and the earth.

Literal Translation.

" The deity being in contemplation, and wishing to create all manner of people out of his own body, first created the waters, and placed in them a seed.

" That (seed) became an egg of golden lustre, as bright as the sun. In this (egg) the Deity himself was born as Brahma the father of all worlds.

" That god, after residing in that egg one year, himself by his own contemplation, broke that egg into two parts.

" With those pieces, he constituted the heaven and the earth. Between (them he created) the visible heavens, the eight cardinal points, and the eternal place of the waters."

Remarks.

Oh People! Observe well what is said in these verses : A seed, which the deity placed in the water, grows into a large egg; the deity, entering into that egg, is born in it as Brahma; Brahma, after lying still for a year, breaks the egg into two parts, and coming forth, establishes one-half of the egg as heaven, and the other half as the earth. How prodigiously absurd is all this! Can we even conceive, that the heavens and the earth were created in this way? How is it that you believe in your Sastras, which relate such absurdities as these?

AN OBJECTION MET.

Some make the following objection. " If the Christian Veda is the true Veda, men will find it out for themselves; why then proclaim it from street to street?"

ANSWER.—This objection is not valid. A toddy shop is among the very worst and most baneful of all things. Yet it is quite needless to publicly proclaim its situation. However secret the place where it is kept, wicked men will surely seek and find it out. Buttermilk, on the other hand, is a most excellent article. Yet this is most properly carried about, and cried from street to street. Just so it is quite unnecessary to publicly preach up a false Sastra; for men, who love falsehood, will certainly seek and find it. But it is eminently proper, on the other hand, that the true Sastra, like good buttermilk, should be preached from street to street.

SCRIPTURE TEXTS.

(1.) The Christian Veda, which is the true Sastra, is not from men, but from God.

2 Peter 1. 21; 2 Tim. 3. 16.

(2.) It is perfect, certain, accurate, holy, true and righteous. It quickens the soul, confers true wisdom, sanctifies the heart, and fills it with joy.

Psalm 19. 7—9; John 17. 17.

(3.) It is a divine torch, which shews the path to heaven.

Psalm 119. 105; Proverbs 6. 22, 24.

(4.) It is a fire that consumes evil dispositions, and a hammer which breaks stony hearts.

Jeremiah 23. 29.

(5.) It is a two-edged sword, which pierces the soul through and through.

Hebrews 4. 12.

(6.) It is rain, which moistens and fructifies the soul.

Isaiah 55. 10, 11.

(7.) It is good seed sown in the heart.

Luke 8. 11, 15.

(8.) It is the power of God unto salvation.

Rom. 1. 16.

(9.) It is more precious than gold, and sweeter than honey.

Psalm 19. 10.

(10.) It can never be destroyed, but is enduring, and certain of fulfilment.

1 Peter 1. 24, 25; Matthew 5. 18.

ADDRESS No. III.

~~~~~~~~~

SIN.

GOD, who is above all, is the Creator, Sustainer and Protector of men. Therefore He is Lord of all. It is His prerogative to lay down the rules by which men are to walk. All without exception are bound to submit to Him, and keep His laws.

God has made known His holy will. He has written His laws on the very hearts of men. All know perfectly well, that lying, and stealing, and murder are wicked deeds. All are fully cognizant, that anger, and covetousness, and lust, and pride, and envy, and hatred are wicked dispositions. And how do they know these things so well? Is it not because God has written on every man's heart the law, that he shall not do these evil deeds, nor indulge these evil dispositions?

More than this: God has promulgated his laws clearly and at large in his holy word of truth. We tell you those laws in the order in which He himself has announced them. Listen. They are ten.

1st. Worship no false gods.
2nd. Bow down to no images.
3rd. Take not the holy name of God in vain.
4th. Keep holy the Sabbath day.
5th. Honor thy father and thy mother.
6th. Do no murder.
7th. Commit not adultery.
8th. Steal not.
9th. Lie not.
10th. Covet not thy neighbor's property.

From these laws it is perfectly plain what sin is. All acts which are in accordance with these divine laws are right. All actions which are opposed to them are wrong.

To the question, whether there is any one in the wide world, who has without failure kept these laws; all must at once reply, that there is no such person. Men do what God has forbidden, and leave undone what he has commanded. And by so doing all are involved in a common ruin.

CUBAL, 47TH CHAPTER; 6TH STANZA.

Translation.

"A man is ruined by doing things which ought not to be done. Equally is he ruined by not doing the things which ought to be done."

In this way, the entire race of men have violated God's laws, and become sinners.

Oh People! Is not this statement strictly true? Look at the actions of men. Many of them, leaving the one only true God, and conceiving certain gods, who have no existence, to be really existent, offer to these purely imaginary beings a vain piety, and a false worship. Many besides setting up and worshipping stocks and stones also raise their joined hands in humble adoration to the cow, the snake, the monkey and the brahmany kite. Many proving faithless to their lawful wives, look upon the faces of strange women. Many steal. Many lie. Many practice all manner of deceits. When we regard the various deeds and transactions of men, as they daily meet our eyes, does it not most evidently appear, that they have all gone out of the way, and are guilty transgressors of the divine laws. As one of your proverbs says, "A mirror is not needed to discover the sore upon one's hand."

Besides the outward and visible actions of men, observe further their inward dispositions. How many the monstrous lusts, which they lovingly cherish within themselves! Instead of accepting God's Law as the rule of their conduct; they proudly reject it, and making a road of their own evil inclinations, blindly pursue it.

Alas! alas! our greatest enemy is this vicious disposition, which we have allowed to take possession of our hearts as its dwelling place.

NEETINERI VILAKKAM, 55.

Translation.

" The wise do not fear external foes, though their number exceed ten millions. But if they discover one internal enemy, they will both fear and guard themselves against it.".

This verse tells us, that wise men do not fear outward enemies, though their number be myriads; but if a single enemy exists within themselves, they are filled with apprehension. Since men have ruined themselves by sinning, their hearts are like an ant-hill, and their wicked dispositions like poisonous snakes, which have crawled into it, and lie there as in their dwelling place. It will not answer to regard these evil dispositions as trifling. Though a snake is very small, it can bite and kill an elephant. So the wicked lust that is within us is able, hissing cobra-like with raised head and expanded hood, to strike and destroy us with the destruction of Hell. The very fact, that such improper desires exist in men's hearts, proves beyond doubt the proposition that they are sinners.

But again: our own consciences bear witness, that we are sinners. You have all heard the proverb, " A guilty conscience twinges, a dirty ear itches." Has not our conscience often reproved us, when we have done wrong? Has it not often said to us, " Oh soul! thou hast sinned; there is a God. He saw your wicked deed. He will judge. He will punish. He will thrust you into hell," and with these words pierced us as with a spear, and wounded us as with a sword? When we transgress, does not our breast throb with pain? Does not our heart burn, when we fall into sin and reproach? Does not a guilty person tremble at the stirring of a mouse, or the rustling of a dry leaf in the wind? Do not men think of the wrongs they have done, when the lightnings flash and the thunders roar? Is it not plain

from these things that conscience powerfully witnesses,
that all men are sinners ?

The Bible tells us, that men are dead in trespasses
and sins.   The meaning of this is, that as a dead body
is destitute of sense and motion, so men are destitute of
holy dispositions and of holy conduct.   As to committing sin, however, far from being like a corpse, they are
full of life and vigor.   Sin is what they desire :   Sin is
what they follow after ; Sin is what they do.

We find the following in one of your poets.

NEETINERI VILAKKAM.

Translation.

" Those, who (while they are ready enough to) eat their
food, smear themselves with ointment, crown themselves
with flowers, and deck themselves with rich clothing, will
yet neither listen to, nor derive instruction from the re-
proofs of the wise, are but breathing corpses."

In other words,

Men crown themselves with flowers ; they rub themselves with unguents ; they deck themselves with fine
clothes ; they eat luxuriously ; in all these matters
they are truly alive ; but if reproved or instructed,
they will give no ear ; they will not open their eyes
to seek the path of virtue.   All such are but breathing
corpses.

Some even among yourselves have discovered and
with tears bewailed the fact, that they were sinners.*

Hear what Tāyumānavar says :—

Literal Translation.

" Oh God most High ! There are none like unto Thee in
the fulness of mercy ; there are none alas ! like unto me in
stoniness of heart."

General Meaning.

As it respects mercy, there are none like unto Thee,
Oh God ! As it respects a hard and wicked heart, there
are alas ! none so bad as I.

* See page 46 of Appendix.

Think not, that you can so hide your sins as to conceal them from God. It is extremely difficult to hide them even from the penetration of shortsighted men. It is of the very nature of sin to come to light.

Observe the following illustration of this found in NEETINERI VILAKKAM, 65 :

Literal Translation.

" However carefully thoroughly decayed and stinking meat may be rolled up and covered with many folds of cloth, its bad odor will diffuse itself, and strike upon the faces even of distant persons. In like manner a guilty word, (or action) however secret the place of its birth, will run and spread far and wide, as though God himself were publishing it by beat of drum."

General Meaning.

However carefully decayed meat may be wrapped up, its bad odor will reach the nostrils of even distant people. So a guilty action will become everywhere manifest, as though God himself published it by beat of drum.

If it be difficult to conceal your sins even from men, how are you going to hide them from the Omniscient God ? Such an attempt would be like trying " to hide a whole pumpkin in a dish of rice." God sees all things. Moreover he is not one, who ever forgets, or ever fails to investigate sinful actions performed.

Oh People ! You have sinned against God, therefore, be afraid. As Tiruvalluvar says :—

CURAL, 21, 2.

Translation.

" Evil actions (done with a view to present happiness afterwards) yield (their legitimate fruit, viz.) calamities. Therefore those evil actions are to be feared more than fire."

The fruit of wicked conduct is the never-ending pain of hell. Remembering then that sin is more cruel than fire, we ought ever to be afraid of it. You commit sin with ease. At the moment of commission, it appears to you in size like a grain of sand. But remembering, that it will hereafter fall upon you with the weight of a mountain and crush you into hell, be startled and tremble both in your bodies and souls.

Beloved! If the sins we have committed are not taken away, the eternal punishment of hell must be our portion. Hence it is necessary, that we should, without delaying, immediately enquire, whether there is any way by which those sins can be removed.

Some tell us, that if we cease to sin, and walk meritoriously, our past sin will thereby be expiated. This is not true. Listen, while we show you this a little in detail.

What is it to walk meritoriously? It is to keep the laws of God always and perfectly, without committing a single fault in thought, word, or deed. Now if any man upon earth could accomplish this, he would be a virtuous man. He would be without sin. He would be entitled to heaven.

But alas! there is no such person upon earth. All men have, times and ways without number, broken God's laws, and committed sin in thought, in word and in deed. Hence all are unquestionably sinners.

If you ask, "But supposing that one who has hitherto sinned were able to break off his sinning, and hereafter to live virtuously, would not his previous sins be thereby removed?" we answer: No, they will not be thereby removed, and for the following reason. Man is bound always to walk virtuously and entirely free from fault. So God himself has ordained. Hence, even if he lead a life in future of spotless virtue, that is no more than what it is his duty to do, and the fulfilment of that duty can in no wise be efficacious to remove a single previous sin. Suppose the case of a man, who has committed a theft. He is bound in future to avoid theft and live honestly. If he does so, he will do only what it is his duty to do, no more and no less. But it is plain, that this will in no wise remove the guilt of his previous theft.

But further, ought we not first of all to inquire whether men have the ability at all to do meritorious actions? Are the deeds, which they extol as meritorious really meritorious? Will God accept them as such? Consider well these questions. We have before proved, that man is a sinner. Being a sinner, from whence is his merit to be derived? Is sin the soil from which merit is to grow? If the water in the spring is bitter, will the water that flows from it be sweet? The inward disposition being sinful, how can the outward deed flowing from such a disposition be meritorious? It is a simple impossibility.

But, some of you will perhaps say, "Surely there are men in the world, who perform many good deeds; are these not to be counted as meritorious?" To this we reply as follows: When you fill a plate with boiled rice, that rice is good. All who see it may truthfully say, "It is delicious food, it is good for hunger, it is in every way most excellent." But let a little arsenic be mixed with that rice; can it then be called good? If any one should proceed to eat it, would not the bystanders immediately warn him saying, "Oh Sir, This has the appearance of being excellent rice, but beware; there is arsenic mixed with it: if you eat it, you will surely die?" Being thus warned, far from calling it good and eating it, he will not even touch it, but will at once reject it as poison. Like that rice, many of the deeds, which men do, have the form and appearance of good deeds. But however good they may appear, their wicked disposition is mixed with those deeds. Whatever the deed done, the man who does it is a sinner. Therefore though his deed appear to the eye, like the rice, good; his evil disposition being mixed with it, it is really like rice poisoned by the admixture of the arsenic. This being so, it is plain, that every action of man is allied with sin; so much so, that he never does and never can do a deed, which, being free from all admixture of sin, is a pure meritorious deed. The truth is, that men are helpless sinners, utterly incapable of performing a really virtuous action. Hence, it is only foolish pride and vain babbling to say, that we can remove and expiate our sins by our meritorious deeds.

Oh People! We can neither hide our sins, nor have we any means by which to remove them. What then shall we do? Do we not need a divine Guru, who shall be able to do virtuous actions possessed of infinite merit? If such a Guru should undertake our case, come into the world, endure to the full in his own person the punishment due to our sins, and do meritorious deeds in our stead, then indeed would our sins be, by him, removed. Unless we find such a Guru, our sins will never be taken away.

Brethren! There is such a sin-destroyer. Jesus Christ is His holy name. The name Jesus means that He is the Savior of the world. The name Christ implies that He is our Prophet, Priest, and King. He and He alone is qualified to instruct us, to remove our sins, to guide us, and to bring us to heaven. He is the true God. It was He who in the beginning created all worlds. It is He, who now sustains and governs all things by His word. It is He who fills the past, the present, and the future. It is He who pervades all space. He the possessor of boundless glory and might left heaven, came into this world, and was born as a man. Thus appearing in this world with two natures, the divine and the human, He lived here during thirty-three years. He walked upon the earth, He spoke, He slept, He rose, He ate. By these and other like actions He shewed himself to be really man He gave eyes to the blind, ears to the deaf, mouths to the dumb, and life to the dead. He taught true wisdom. He made the way to heaven. By these and other similar deeds, He proved himself to be really God.

He was most gracious to all who approached him. He blessed even infants. Himself leading a life of perfect holiness, He clearly exemplified the holy rule of life by which men ought to walk. He reproved men's transgressions. He taught, that men must feel their sin, mourn over it, forsake it, turn unto God, and lead lives of faith and uprightness. But men, being in love with their sins, not only rejected His good teaching, but were filled with hatred against Him. They plotted to kill him. Although he perceived their design, He did not destroy them, but gave Himself up to them. They laid their wicked hands upon Him. Placing Him on a cross, they fixed him to it with nails. Hanging there, He died. The Sun hid his face unable to endure the sight. Darkness filled the entire land. Rocks rent asunder. The earth quaked and trembled. After death he was placed in a tomb. But on the third day, bursting the bonds of death, which He had himself assumed, He rose alive from the grave. He appeared to many persons. He commanded his disciples to go the world over, and preach His death, and the salvation secured by it to every creature. Finally He ascended up through the air, and re-entered the world of heaven from whence He had come. While He was ascending; the angels of God, coming forth from heaven, met and worshipped Him. Then, as if festooning the sky with triumphant garlands, they gathered in shining ranks before and behind, above and below Him, and thus arrayed accompanied his progress with songs of praise and adoration. There He now sits in glory as the Ruler of all worlds.

If you ask why he consented to die, the answer is; He did so in order that He might bear and remove the sins of men. It was for this very purpose, that He came to earth. He frequently announced this purpose beforehand. Hear one saying of his : " No man taketh it (my life) from me, but I lay it down of myself. I have power to lay it down and I have power to take it again: this commandment have I received of my Father."* Having thus announced beforehand, that, in order to save the world He would sacrifice His life, die, and rise again on the third day, He, in accordance with this, gave Himself up of His own will to the death of the cross.

The death of Jesus Christ is the true atoning sacrifice. Atonement implies the complete removal of sin. The shedding in behalf of sinners of His holy blood by

* John 10, 18.

Jesus Christ, who is the very incarnation of all merit, is the one only real expiatory sacrifice. This alone will avail. His death is our refuge. It is the tree, which produces for us the eternal fruit of heavenly joy.

This will appear from what follows. The death which He endured was the punishment He bore in our behalf. That the punishment of hell might not fall on us, He came to earth, and was punished thus in our stead. If you ask, whether the punishment which He suffered upon earth was an equivalent to the eternal suffering, which we deserve to endure in hell; we reply, that it was. Is not a single stroke inflicted upon the back of a king a far greater punishment than an hundred inflicted upon the back of a common cooly? Undoubtedly it is. Yet both the cooly and the king are equally but men. If there be such disparity as this among men, what shall we say of the distance in the same respect between a man and God? Must it not be infinite? We are but insignificant men : Jesus Christ is the eternal God. Is it not clear then, that the suffering which he endured upon earth is not merely an equivalent of the punishment due to us, but that it infinitely surpasses and exceeds that punishment?

Oh people ! Consider this with attention and candor. Is there anywhere to be found such merit as this of Jesus Christ, the Redeemer of the world, who for our sakes was born upon earth, led a life of spotless purity, and finally gave himself up to death itself? Is it not unspeakable, inconceivable, boundless ! Those who believe in this Savior obtain by His merit the removal of their sins, and, thus escaping hell, reach and enter the world of heaven. This, and this only, is the way of expiation.

But perhaps you will still further inquire as to the cause of his having thus suffered and died? Oh Brethren ! let your hearts melt, when we tell you that it was love, and love alone. He could gain no profit, no emolument from us. But moved by infinite love, He was filled with irresistible desire to liberate and rescue us from eternal ruin and torment. His grace is broader than the ocean, higher than heaven, deeper than hell. Therefore it was, that he came to save us.

Let me illustrate this. There is a mother, whose infant is stricken with a fatal disease. The physician attending addresses the mother as follows: "Madam, this is a serious malady. If I administer the proper remedy for it, the child cannot bear it, but will die. You however can take the medicine. Entering into your blood, it will become commingled with your milk, and with it gushing from your breasts into the mouth of your child, will save its life and restore it to health. But I warn you beforehand, that the medicine will occasion you great bodily distress. It will produce a torture like the breaking of your bones. The pain will be all yours; the benefit, all your child's." Will the mother on hearing this refuse, think you, to take the medicine? Will she stop even to consider whether to take it or no? Will she not rather eagerly acquiesce saying, "Oh Doctor! Is not this the child I carried in my womb for ten long months? It is my jewel, my eye. Give me quickly the medicine of which you speak. If it kills me, let it kill me. I will take it with joy?" And will she not at once seize and swallow the remedy? And Oh! who can tell the joy she would experience, when after having taken the medicine, borne the torture, and snatched her babe from the jaws of death, she looks upon it restored to life and health? And the child too, when it has grown up, and learns of its mother's self-sacrificing love, think you it will not love her in return? And now is it needful to ask the question, why the mother took the medicine, and why she exposed herself to such suffering? If such a question should be asked, one short sentence will answer it fully. "She did it from love." Brethren! Listen attentively. We are that little babe. The sin we have committed is the disease, that has seized upon us. The punishment of hell, which is sin's fruit, is the ruin in which we are about to be plunged. It is an eternal, never-ending ruin. The divine Guru, Jesus Christ, is to us in the place of the mother. As the mother of the illustration gladly took and experienced in her own person the torture her infant could not survive; so Jesus Christ took upon himself and bore all the punishment due to our sins. As the babe seized upon the mother's breast, so we must lay hold upon Jesus Christ with faith and love. As it drank the medicine incorporated with its mother's milk, so we thinking of the pains which Jesus Christ endured for us, should, with dissolving hearts, mourn over our sins, abhor them, and repent. Then, as that infant gained health and lived and prospered; so we, obtaining the bliss of heaven, will be for ever happy. Oh Brethren? How can you ask the question, why Christ suffered for us? Tell us why that mother suffered for her child, and we will answer your question in the same words.

Throw away all your vain objections. Hear what Tāyumānavar says,

Translation.

"Oh thou, who art infinitely more gracious than the mother who bore me! Shall I ever see the day, when my soul, meditating on Thy love, shall dissolve into tenderness like wax that has fallen into the fire."

Make these words your own, and praying that God, more gracious than the mothers who bore you, will cause your hearts to melt this very hour, believe on Jesus Christ as your Saviour, and join His holy religion without delay.

APPENDIX TO No. III.

EXAMPLES AND ILLUSTRATIONS.

(1.) A sorrowful lamentation, shewing that we are sinners.

Brahmans recite this Sloka every day while performing their ablutions.

Literal Translation.

"I am possessor of sin; I am one who does sin;
I am a sinful soul; I was born with sin;
Oh God! who art gracious to those seeking refuge,
Save me by grace."

General Meaning.

Alas! I am a sinner; all my actions are sinful; my soul is filled with sin; I was born in sin. Oh Lord! Oh God! most merciful to those, who seek refuge in Thee: Save me by Thy grace.

ANOTHER SLOKA.

Literal Translation.

" Sins a thousand are committed day and night by me. Oh God! remembering that I am (Thy) servant, forgive."

General Meaning.

The sins which I commit by night and by day are thousands upon thousands. Oh God! accepting me as Thy servant, graciously pardon my transgressions.

ANOTHER SLOKA.

Literal Translation.

" Among sinners, I am the chief. Among the gracious Thou art the pre-eminent. Who else is there in these three worlds, who more than I stands in need of Thy grace?"

General Meaning.

Oh God! I am the chief of sinners: Thou art pre-eminent among the gracious. Is there any one in all the three worlds, who needs Thy grace more than I do?

SCRIPTURE TEXTS.

(1.) The nature of sin.
    1 John 3. 4.

(2.) All men are sinners.
    Romans 3. 10, 18.
    This is apparent,

(a.) From their actions.
    Rom. 1. 29, 32.
    Gal. 5. 19, 21.
    2 Tim. 3. 2, 5.
    Titus 3. 3.

(b.) From their dispositions.
    Mark 7. 20, 23.
    Rom. 8. 7.
    Jer. 17. 9.

(c.) From the testimony of their consciences.

Rom. 2. 15.

Gen. 42. 21, 22.

(3.) Men are dead in trespasses and sins.

Eph. 2. 1, 3.

(4.) It is impossible to hide sin, so that God shall not see it.

Heb. 4. 13.

Psalm 90. 8.

Jer. 23, 24.

(5.) Men should be alarmed because they have sinned.

1 Cor. 6. 9, 10.

Mat. 13. 40, 42.

Rev. 21. 8.

Psalm 9. 7.

(6.) Men are incapable of meritorious actions.

Job 14. 4.

Job 25. 4, 6.

Isaiah 6. 4, 6.

Rev. 3, 17, 18.

(7.) We need a divine Guru who is able to perform deeds of infinite merit.

Jer. 33. 16.

1 Cor. 1. 30.

1 John 2. 2.

ADDRESS No. IV.

MAN.

WHEN we observe man's constitution, we find that he has a body and that he has a soul.

It is manifest to all, that the body is mortal. It is composed of the five elements. He who created those five elements, and united them to form the body is God. At death, He will disunite them. Then the body will be resolved back into the five elements, which compose it. The earth in the body will return to earth. The water in it will mix with water. The air that ranges through it will fly away with the air. Thus, at death, this body will be dissolved and scattered.

That our body is not enduring and will speedily decay is a common observation.

Hear what Pattanattu Pillai sings,

Literal Translation.

If you ask what the body is,

" It is silk cotton piled up in the wind; it is the multitude of dew drops before the morning Sun; it is the rainbow which appears in the sky; it is the fleeting shadow of a thunder-cloud."

General Meaning.

As cotton which flies before the gale; as a dew drop which melts away at sight of the Sun; as the bow of heaven, which fades as soon as it appears; as the shadow of a cloud fleeting over the earth; so man's body stops not here, but quickly passes away.

Man has a soul in addition to the body. The body is like a house. The house will crumble into ruins. But there is one who inhabits this house. He is the soul. He crumbles not with his house. This soul has no affinity with the five elements. Earth, air, fire, water and ether do not enter into the composition of the soul. The soul is incapable of separating into fragments or particles. It cannot fall as earth. It cannot flow as water. It cannot flame forth as fire. It cannot fly away as wind. It cannot commingle with ether. This soul is without form. It will never perish. It will never part with its essence, but endure for ever the same.

This soul, which is the lord of the body, is a substance endowed with intelligence. It recognises the distinction between sin and merit. It weighs good and evil. It knows God. Moreover this soul reads books. It examines and apprehends the meaning of Sastras. It ponders what is past, what is present, and what is future. It contemplates the unseen worlds of heaven and hell. It dreads a future state of misery, it craves a future state of happiness. Our soul is possessed of all these powers and capacities.

If you ask, "This being so, is this soul itself the Deity ?" we reply, " By no means." Some persons in this country, acting under the insane delusions of a vain pride, do, it is true, affirm that God and our souls are one and the same.* This is a prodigious infatuation. God and our souls are substances entirely distinct from each other. He is the self-existent Soul without 'origin or beginning ; our soul was made by Him. He is the Infinite Supreme Soul ; we are but finite created souls. He is Omnipresent, filling all space ; our soul is confined to a limited place. He knows all things ; the knowledge possessed by our souls is insignificant. He is Omnipotent, the Creator of heaven and of earth ; our soul has but a trifle of power, it cannot create even an atom of sand. He is above and over all ; our soul is at His disposal and direction. Since such differences as these exist, it is certain that our soul is not God.†

* See Appendix, page 60.

† See Appendix, page 60.

To say that God and man's soul are one and the same substance is not only opposed to reason, but is also blasphemy. Those who teach this doctrine are founders and abettors of immorality. If men are taught, that, whatever they may do, the deed is not theirs, but God's; they will of course venture fearlessly into the commission of sin. All wicked and lewd persons will naturally extol such doctrine as excellent, in words like these; " This truly is the perfection of instruction. Indeed it is quite faultless. Let the wickedness be ever so atrocious, we may do it without fear. It will in no case be our deed; but God's deed." So saying, they will commit the most flagitious immorality with unchecked appetite and joy. Should such doctrine become universally prevalent, the earth would at once be filled with violence, and becoming unsettled would be utterly destroyed. Can this doctrine, which would cause immorality and vice to increase indefinitely, be true? It is not true. It is a lie of boundless dimensions. It is a false doctrine, fitted only to make a hell upon earth. Therefore, reject and clear your minds entirely of this infamous tenet. The soul is not God, neither will it ever become God.

Our soul is destined to leave the body and pass away. There is no device, by which our life can be tied to its temporary habitation. Suppose the case of a man, who wishes to preserve unbroken a bubble floating on the water. Imagine him making iron rings, and carefully fastening them around it by way of securing the end in view. Will he succeed think you? Will not the bubble soon burst, and the air it contains fly away? Now however ardently we may strive, like the man putting iron rings around the bubble, to preserve this body of ours by feeding, clothing and administering medicine, we know that it cannot remain permanently upon the earth. Do what we may, it will soon die, and the soul now within it will go out of it and pass away. Death comes to all. Old and young must without exception die. However many days we may live upon earth; our body is sure at last to reach its destination, either on the funeral pile or in six feet of earth.

If you ask, " When the soul will leave the body and pass away ?" that is known to none in this world. All we can say is, that it will do so at death. But no one can beforehand determine and declare the time when death will come. " Can man know the future as he does the past ?"

Tāyumānavar, one of your own poets, says,

" There is no assured ground of thinking that those born to-day will be to-morrow alive."

Again; when the soul departs from the body, what will it carry away with it ? Let Tāyumānavar answer the question.

Literal Translation.

" Will the spacious mansion, the wife, the child, the prosperity, the stored up wealth accompany the precious soul, when it quits the body and passes away ?"

General Meaning.

When the body dies, will the spacious mansion, the lovely wife, the beloved child, the cherished comfort, and the accumulated wealth accompany the departing soul ? Alas! no one of them all.

For as Pattanattu Pillai says,

" Not even an eyeless needle will accompany (us) in the last journey."

However much one may accumulate in this world, his soul cannot take up and carry away with it even a straw. The riches of earth are diverse in nature from the soul, and hence cannot adhere to it. But sin and merit are affiliated with the soul, and therefore will accompany it in its departure from the world.

So says the same Pattanattu Pillai.

Literal Translation.

" Wealth and prosperity will remain in the house. Sorrowing women, with love-floods streaming from their eyes will come as far as the street. Weeping sons, sobbing bitterly

with both hands placed on their heads, will accompany even
to the place of cremation. The two moral actions of good and
evil alone will adhere to and follow (the departing soul.)"

General Meaning.

When one dies, his wealth will remain within his
house. His mother, wife and other female relatives,
coming with him as far as the street, will stop there.
His children will accompany him to the burning place,
but they can go no farther. Beyond that spot, nothing
but his sins and his merits can be his companions. So
says the verse just quoted. Oh people! Men are all
sinful souls. There is not one single meritorious
soul among them. If while still alive upon the earth,
they believe in Jesus Christ the Saviour of the world,
they will receive the merits of that Saviour as their own;
and thus, being freed from sin, will at death depart from
the body as meritorious souls. If while in the world,
they do not lay hold upon that Saviour; they must at
death go forth from their bodies, encumbered with their
sins as sinful souls. There is nothing that our souls can
take away with them as their own from this world
except one of these two; *viz.*, either the sin we have
committed in this life, or the merit conferred on us by
Jesus Christ. This is a true saying.

But where will the soul go, when separated from the
body? Will it, reaching a good state, live happily; or will
it, reaching a bad state, be plunged into sorrow? This is
what we all chiefly need to know. Many among you
say, that the departed soul will pass through numerous
births. Is this worthy of belief? Can we for a moment
suppose, that the human soul, losing its very nature,
will be born and die successively in the form of a cow,
a monkey, a snail, a fish, a bird, an insect, a tree, a
creeper, a grass, a stone, a piece of dirt, and thus go on
for ages, rolling and tumbling over and over from one
birth and death to another indefinitely? Surely such
teaching as this is worthy only of ridicule and rejection.
The soul of man has never yet, bereft of its human
nature, been born either as beast, fish, bird, worm or

plant; and, what is more, it will never be so born in the future. Man is born but once, and he dies but once upon earth.

This being so, you will ask, "Where then does our soul go at death?" The Bible alone gives an answer to this question. Listen attentively while we tell it to you.

That this matter may become clear, know first of all that there are three worlds, and listen as we enter into some particulars about them.

In the firmament above us is the world of Heaven. There God displays His glory and His grace. It is a world of light, where darkness never comes. It is a holy world, in which sin has never placed its foot. It is a happy abode, which knows neither pain nor sorrow. In it there is no hunger, no disease, no decrepitude, no death, no hate, no revenge. Those who reach that world will see God, and enjoy His favor. They will experience the comforts of supreme felicity. They will shine for ever in the presence of God. The happiness and transcendent excellence of that world is beyond the reach not only of words, but of our imaginations.

In the abyss below us is the world of Hell. There dwell fiends, goblins and devils. Satan, the king of evil spirits, sways over it the sceptre of a cruel despot. Hell is a world of gloom, covered over with densest darkness. It is an unholy place, filled with sin and uncleanness. It is an abode of pain and anguish and crowding afflictions. In it there is neither health, friendship nor joy. It is fitly named a lake of fire. Those who reach this world will become eternal slaves to devils. They will be tormented by fiends. Bereft of every comfort, they will endure never-ending punishment. There they will stay for ever and ever, sobbing and weeping, beating their breasts and gnashing their teeth in anguish inconceivable. The distress and ignominy of hell no tongue can tell, no thought can comprehend.

Between these two worlds is our Earth. In it we remain for a few days, experiencing by turn joy and sorrow, prosperity and adversity. If now it be asked,

" where does our soul go, when, after casting its body into dust and ashes, it passes away from this world ?" the answer is ; It goes either to the world of heaven, or to the world of hell. Into whichever world it then enters, in that world it must eternally remain. Hence the necessity of our immediately and earnestly seeking the way by which we may escape going to hell, and gain access to heaven. This should be to us in this life our greatest concern, and chiefest effort.

Is it not sheer madness* to labor and toil continuously for this dying body, while we neglect seeking a happy state for our deathless souls ? Is it wise to eat the skin, and throw the fruit as useless to the crows ? Is it reasonable to preserve the shell, and cast the pearl into the dunghill ? Hear what one of your poets says :

ARA-NERI-SARAM.

Literal Translation.

" The days that are passed may all be counted by placing (the thumb) on the other fingers. Reflecting that the days yet to come are beyond any one's computation ; how great is his folly, who without doing any good suffers his time to pass away unimproved !"

General Meaning.

Few are the days that have passed away. They may all be counted with the thumb upon the fingers. But no one can compute the days that are yet to come. Hence it is the height of folly for a man to suffer his remaining days upon earth to fleet away unimproved by any effort to accomplish good.

It being certain, that one or the other of these two worlds, viz., heaven and hell, must be our final destination ; it becomes us to inquire and ascertain what class of souls will rise to heaven, and what class of souls will fall into hell. God has revealed this most clearly. The souls of those, whose sin is removed on this earth, will at the time of death enter the world of heaven. The souls of those, whose sin is not removed on this earth,

* See Appendix, page 60.

will at the time of death go into the world of hell. Since this is so, it is above all things necessary for us to ascertain how sin can be removed, and how the soul can obtain merit. However much men may investigate these questions with their own reason, they will never be able to solve them. The sins we have committed are sins against God. Who then but God Himself can reveal to us the means whereby the sin, which we have, can be removed; and the merit, which we have not, can be acquired? To acquaint us with this, God has graciously given His holy word. We proceed to tell you, what that true Sastra reveals. Listen attentively.

We are utterly incapable either of removing our sins, or of acquiring merit. But there is a mighty one who is perfectly competent to do both these things for us. That one is Jesus Christ, the Son of God. He and He alone is the Lord of all creation, and the Saviour of the whole world. Wishing to redeem men's souls from sin, He left heaven and, descending to earth, became incarnate as a man. He dwelt in this world thirty-three years. Wherever He went His grace shone out resplendent. He did good to all. He caused the blind to see, the deaf to hear, the dumb to speak. He restored lepers, and others afflicted with similar great and incurable diseases, to perfect health. He gave life to the hopelessly dead. He routed devils and fiends. He subdued raging winds, and roaring seas. He did all these wonders by His almighty word. By the miracles He performed in each of them, heaven, earth and sea united in bearing witness, that God, the sovereign Lord of them all, had come into this world the Guru and Redeemer of man.

Besides these benefits done to the bodies of men, Jesus Christ taught true doctrine for the good of their souls. Nay more than this, He consented Himself to bear our sin. We, who have sinned, are the guilty ones. It is upon us, that the punishment of sin ought to be inflicted. But He, who was without guilt, assuming our guilt as his own, bore the punishment in our stead. For our sakes, He suffered untold humiliation upon earth. Abuse and reproaches were heaped upon Him. He was nailed to the cross. He shed his holy blood. He yielded up even His life for us. Reviving again on the third day, He rose from the tomb, and appeared upon the earth. Thus he bore and expiated our sins. Finally, having commanded His disciples to go into all the world, and preach Him as the Saviour, He left this earth, and returned to heaven.

Since this Jesus Christ, who was born a man for the benefit of man, has fulfilled all the laws of God in our stead, and has also borne the punishment due to our sins; it is plain, that He has procured for us a store of infinite merit. That Christ-procured merit is the sinners' only refuge.

Oh People! The sins of all those, who obtain the merit of Jesus Christ, are at once removed. They need not fear to die. Christ's merit will go along with their departing souls. It will open wide the gates of heaven before them. It will lodge them safely in that world of bliss. But all such as do not obtain, while here on earth, the merits of Christ, will together with their load of sin, assuredly sink into the depths of hell.

Do you ask how we may obtain His merits? We must believe in Him. That is the only way. Address Him in prayer with such words as these: "Oh Jesus Saviour! I have committed much sin. I have deeply offended against Thee. This is my distress, this my sorrow. I can no longer consent to sin, and walk in opposition to Thee. I seek refuge in Thee. Thou hast borne my punishment. Thou hast expiated my sin. Believing, I cling to Thee alone. The blood Thou spilledst is the only sacred bathing-place for my soul. Thy holy feet are my only asylum. Rejecting all other ways, I will walk in the way which Thou hast taught. Mercifully receive me. Graciously remit my sins. Grant me Thy Holy Spirit, and make my heart pure. Create true piety within me, and make me walk in the good way." Trusting thus in Him as your only God and Guru, lay fast hold of Him. If you come truly believing to Jesus Christ, He will never repulse you. On the contrary, He will graciously receive you as His own, bless you, pardon your sins, give you His own merits as an everlasting inheritance, and save you for ever. Thus you will be assured of heaven's eternal bliss.

Oh People! Hear another most important truth. The Lord Jesus Christ, who ascended to heaven, will come again to this earth. The time of His return is named the day of Judgment. In that day, He will come with divine glory accompanied by myriads of holy angels. At sight of Him, the sun will be darkened, and the moon turned into blood. The stars will fall, and the heaven will pass away. Great and terrible will that day be.

In that day, all the souls, who obtaining while upon earth remission of their sins by Jesus Christ have ascended into heaven, will with Him come forth from that blissful world. In that day all the souls, who, with their load of guilt, have fallen from earth into hell, will, at the command of Jesus Christ, in like manner, come forth from that world of despair. Then will Christ in the twinkling of an eye raise up the bodies of all these souls, both those which came forth from heaven, and those which came forth from hell. Each soul will at that moment receive again the very body, which it had while upon the earth, and all will be made to stand in the presence of Jesus Christ. Oh Brethren, what an immense concourse that will be! All men, who from the beginning to the end of the world have been born and died upon it, in all times and in all countries, will without a single exception stand together there a countless multitude. Then Jesus Christ, the Lord and Judge of all, will proceed to judge them. Everything that men thought and said and did, while living upon this earth, will, on this judgment-day, be brought to light, and sentence will be pronounced upon each one according to his deeds. Jesus Christ will divide that vast multitude into two parts. All those who while upon earth believ-

ed in Him, and obtained from Him the remission of
their sins, He will on that day place on His right hand.
All others He will station on His left. Then He will
pronounce judgment. Saying to those on His left hand,
" Depart from me ye cursed into everlasting fire," He
will cast their soul and body into hell, and fasten its
gates upon them. From that place they will never escape and come forth. There they will suffer eternal
torments. Casting a gracious loving eye upon those
standing on his right hand, and saying, " Come ye blessed and inherit the kingdom," He will gather them with
their bodies into heaven. There they will enjoy eternal
felicity. Between heaven and hell will for ever be
fixed a gulph great and impassable to all.

Beloved ! lay these things to your hearts. Come to
Jesus the Redeemer of the world. Time flies rapidly
away. Death and Judgment draw swiftly near. Waste
not vainly your days. This world's good is not enduring. Your abode is not enduring. Parents and relatives
are not enduring. Beauty, grandeur and wealth are
not enduring. The sacred feet of Christ the heavenly
Guru alone are enduring.

Pāmbātti Sittar says,

" As the bubble which forms on the water bursts and is
gone, so the body will speedily pass away. Reflecting upon
this as certain, relinquish oh my soul ! all attachment to
worldly things, and laying hold upon, cling only to him who
created the earth and all living souls."

Weigh well the meaning of these words. Remembering ever, that your body must soon pass away, like a
bubble on the water, seek not earth's perishable riches ;
but lay fast hold of the Creator and Saviour of souls.

Brethren ! Jesus Christ alone is the Lord, who is the
Creator and All-mighty Redeemer of souls. Other
Saviour there is none. Now is your opportunity. Seek
refuge in Him without delay.*

* See Appendix, page 61.

APPENDIX to No. IV.

ILLUSTRATIONS AND EXAMPLES.

(1.)   Concerning the false doctrine that God and the soul of man are one and the same.

A Sloka has been invented among the Hindus to set forth this mischievous doctrine.   We are told, that it is embodied in the Sama Veda, and that it is called the "Maha Vakya."   It is as follows :—

Literal Translation.

" Thou art That."

General Meaning.

Thou my soul ! art the universal soul, that is, God.

Of all lies this is the greatest lie ; of all frauds, this is the worst fraud.   To call this a "Maha Vakya" is the merest childishness.

(2.)   Sanscrit Sloka, affirming that God and the soul of man are not one and the same.

Literal Translation.

" By the difference of wisdom universal and wisdom infinitesimal ; by (the difference of) power universal and power infinitesimal ; by (the difference of independence and dependence, God and the soul are not one."

General Meaning.

God is Omniscient, man's soul has but little knowledge ; therefore the two are not one.   God is Almighty, man's soul has but trifling power ; therefore the two are not one.   God is over all independent, man's soul is subject to and dependent on God ; therefore the two are not one.

(3.)   Example affirming, that to neglect seeking heaven, while slaving daily for a dying body, is folly.

Literal Translation.

" Oh Vamana ; men upon earth toil always and continuously for the body which is not eternal ; but they toil not at any time to gain the eternal bliss of heaven."

General Meaning.

Oh Vamana! Men toil evermore for this mortal fleeting body; but they take no pains to gain heaven, which is Eternal.

(4.) Sanscrit Sloka affirming that the soul's salvation should be sought without delay.

Literal Translation.

"Let (man) do good to his soul (now) while this body is well, and death still distant! what can he do in the hour of dissolution?"

General Meaning.

Let each one seek the good of his soul while his body is still healthful, and death still far away; for what can he do, when he shall lie sick and at the point of death?

SCRIPTURE TEXTS.

(1.) The body is not eternal:
Life is a shadow.
Job 8. 9.
It is as grass and as the flower of grass.
Psalm 103. 15, 16.
1 Peter 1. 24, 25.
Dust will return to dust.
Genesis 3. 19.

(2.) The soul is imperishable.
Ecclesiastes 12. 7.

(3.) God and the soul of man are not one:
God created the soul.
Zechariah 12. 1.
God is without bounds.
1 Chronicles 29. 11.

(4.) It is beyond our power to keep the soul in the body:
Ecclesiastes 8. 8.

(5.) What will accompany the soul departing at death:
Worldly wealth will not accompany it.
Ecclesiastes 5. 15.
1 Timothy 6. 7.

r

Christ's merits will accompany the believer.
Psalm 23. 4.
1 Thess. 5. 10.
Romans 14. 8.
His own sin will accompany the sinner.
Ezekiel 3. 19.
John 8. 24.

(6.)   The three worlds:
Heaven;
A world of light filled with divine glory.
Rev. 21. 23.
A world of holiness.
Rev. 21. 27.
A world of bliss.
Psalm 16. 11.
A world free from all distress.
Rev. 7. 16, 17.
Rev. 21. 4.
Those reaching it will see God.
Rev. 22. 4.
They will have everlasting joy.
Isaiah 51. 11.
They will shine.
Mat. 13. 43.
Hell;
A world where devils and fiends dwell.
Mat. 25. 41.
A world covered with the darkness of impurity
and distress.
Mat. 22. 13.
A lake of fire.
Rev. 20. 15.
Those going there will be tormented.
Luke 16. 24.
They will weep and wail and gnash their teeth.
Mat. 13. 50.
Earth;
In the day of Christ's coming, the earth, and
its works will be consumed.
2 Peter 3. 10, 11.

(7.) At death the soul will enter either heaven or hell.

Luke 16. 22, 23.

(8.) Toiling for the mortal body, and neglecting to seek a happy state for the immortal soul is folly.

Luke 12. 16 to 21.

(9.) He whose sins are not removed will at death fall into hell. He who has been justified by the merits of Christ will at death ascend to heaven.

Prov. 14. 32.

Mat. 25. 46.

(10.) The Judgment day :

Christ will come to judge.

Mat. 25. 31.

1 Thess. 4. 16.

The sun will be darkened, the stars will fall, and other wonders take place.

Rev. 6. 12 to 17.

Christ will raise all the dead.

John 5. 28, 29.

All will be arraigned before Him.

Rev. 20. 12.

2 Cor. 5. 10.

All the actions of men while upon earth will on that day be brought to light.

Ecclesiastes 12. 14.

Matthew 12. 36.

Christ will divide that vast multitude into two classes.

Matthew 25. 32, 33.

Those on His left hand will be cast into Hell.

Matthew 25. 41.

Those on His right hand will be gathered into Heaven.

Matthew 25. 34.

There is a great impassable gulph fixed between Heaven and Hell.

Luke 16. 26.

ADDRESS No. V.

GOD.

Oh People! you say, that Brahma and Vishnu and Siva are gods. This is a common remark in this country; and you, without ever inquiring whether it is true or false, accept it as right, and believe that Triad* to be really god. Now is it the part of wise men thus to do? Is it reasonable to believe everything we hear, without once examining as to its truth or falsity? Does not he incur great dangers, who without investigation accepts as true each prevailing rumor? You know the proverb which says that,

"Inconsiderate action ends in incurable sorrow?"
Now to believe in and follow the true God is the highest happiness we are capable of. But who can describe the measure of our ruin; if, forsaking Him, we follow after false gods? Therefore we earnestly entreat you to inquire a little into the affairs of these three persons, whom you call gods.

We shall now quote what is said of them in your own Sastras. Let those Sastras be their witnesses; and do you, carefully sifting and weighing the evidence they bear, give just judgment in the cases brought before you.

BRAHMA'S CASE.

Skanda Purana : Markanda Padala.

Literal Translation.

"We are not ignorant of the story, that Brahma, whose dwelling of old is the matchless lotus flower, having created skilfully with his own hands the gazelle-eyed Tilōttamai to be peerless queen of beauty among the bevy of damsels with

---

* For the conflicting statements of the Sastras, as to which one of the Triad is the greatest; see Appendix, pages 77, 78, 79 and 80.

foreheads like the crescent moon, gazed upon her bewitching countenance, and became four-faced, coveting her charms."

From this stanza it appears, that Brahma lusted after his daughter, whom he had himself created ; and that, when she affrighted fled from his wicked solicitations, he assumed four faces to discover where she was.

Hear now a Cural, sung by Tiruvalluvar, about adultery.

CURAL, 15TH CHAPTER ; 2ND STANZA.

Literal Translation.

" Among all, who stand in (the ways of) sin ; there are no fools greater than those, who stand at their neighbour's door, (lusting after his wife)."

General Meaning.

Among the worst of sinners, there is no greater sinner, than he, who stands at the door of another man, lusting after his wife.

If desiring the wife of another is a folly so extreme, and a sin so heinous ; who can express the guilt and reproach of Brahma, the debaucher of his own daughter?

This being so, it is plain that, according to the rule laid down by your own Tiruvalluvar, Brahma, far from being a god, is nothing other than a sinner and a fool. To say, that such an one is Creator of the Universe, is more like a ribald jest than any thing else.

VISHNU'S CASE.

B'HAGAVATA : 10TH SKANDHA : SAGADAMUTAITTA AD'HYAYA.

Literal Translation.

" Krishna looses the young calves, which are tied : he seizes and devours the curds mingled with butter : climbing up on the mortar, he stretches out his hand and grasps the articles suspended on the lofty roof-rope : flinging (stones and sticks) he breaks what he cannot thus reach."

General Meaning.

In this stanza, the shepherdesses are represented as making complaint against Krishna to his mother Asōdai thus, "Oh Asōdai! This Krishna is continually untying and letting loose our young calves, which are tied; he eats up all our butter and curds; when he cannot reach the roof-rope, he puts the mortar under it, and climbing up, stretches out his hand, and takes every thing suspended on it; and if he does not succeed in that way, he breaks the pots by throwing sticks and stones at them, and then gathers up and carries off what they spill."

It is further related of Krishna, that besides thus going from house to house, and stealing milk, curds, butter-milk and butter; he was, on account of his thefts, tied on one occasion to a mortar and well beaten.

Now hear what Tiruvalluvar says of theft:

CURAL, 29TH CHAPTER; 2ND STANZA.

Literal Translation.

"Even the thought (of wrong) is sin; Say not then, 'we will craftily steal another's property.'"

General Meaning.

Do not even think of stealing another's possessions; for the very thought of such a crime is a great sin.

According then to this rule, laid down by your own Tiruvalluvar; Vishnu is not a god, but only a great sinner.

But we have not done yet; for according to your own Sastras, Krishna, besides committing the sins before-mentioned, also ravished many shepherdesses; he defrauded the emperor Mahābali; he, after giving his word not to use weapons in the war of the B'hārata, took up arms and violated his promise; and he ruthlessly murdered the washerman of his uncle Kansa. These are only a few of his misdeeds. To undertake to relate here all the crimes he committed would cover too much space. It is enough for you to know, that his deeds prove him to be an unparalleled villain.

But some apologise by saying, that Vishnu did these things only in his incarnations. Surely this is a worthless excuse. God is eternally holy. He is one, who cannot, under any circumstances whatever, fall into sin. Hence the admission, that Vishnu sinned even in his incarnations, proves him a sinner and no god. Not only so; but the very incarnations, which you say he assumed, far from being divine, are thereby demonstrated to be only spurious.

But again, Vishnu committed infamous crimes, when he was not incarnate. Let a single example taken from your Sastras suffice. Vishnu, on one occasion, when not in any of his incarnations, assuming the form of the nymph Mōhini, went and standing before Siva captivated him by the exhibition of various obscene and lascivious gestures. We leave the story with this bare mention of it, because its details are too indecent to be cited.

Oh People! How is it, that you can consent to acknowledge and worship this Vishnu as a god? Answer yourselves, whether it is the nature of God to be a thief, a debauché, a liar and a murderer?

You affirm, that Vishnu is the sovereign Protector of the Universe. But Vishnu, in accordance with the proverb,

" Once a thief, always a thief," *

stole butter and other household productions from many people. This being so, does it not sound very much like drollery to say, that he is the sovereign Protector of all things?

SIVA'S CASE.

SKANDA PURANA: UTTAPADALA.

Literal Translation.

" Can the reproach ever be removed from Siva, who, in the form of a mendicant carrying in his beautiful hand an

* The Tamil proverb literally translated runs thus : Although a thief be in a dark house, his thievish hand will not leave him. The meaning is, A thief will steal under all circumstances.

alms-vessel, violated the wives of the Rishis, living in this
Tārugāvanam ? It will spread in every quarter where the
Sun and Moon shine."

General Meaning.

This stanza tells us, that Siva, taking the form of a
handsome mendicant, and bearing an alms-vessel in his
hand, entered Tārugāvanam, and violated the chastity
of the wives of the Rishis, living in that place.

It is further related in the Skanda Purana, which is
an acknowledged Sivite authority, that Siva committed
many other sins. He played at dice with Parvati; and
when he was defeated, he lied saying, that he had not
lost but won the game. Then addressing Parvati, he
said, " As you have lost, hand over to me the jewels you
staked on the play."

Again ; Siva, on another occasion, gazing upon
Mōhini, the female form which Vishnu had assumed,
lusted after her and committed indecencies, which will
not bear relating.

Listen now to a dictum of Siva, contained in the Mahā
B'harata, concerning such deeds.

NALLA PILLAI B'HARATA : ANUSASANIKA PARUVAM :
UMAMAKESVARA SAMVATAM.

Literal Translation.

" The matchless three-eyed Siva, (addressing Pārvati,)
said ; Oh chaste Vine ! know that he, whose nature it is with
honeyed tongue to labor for the procurement to himself of
another's property, or another's wife, will fall into the abyss
of hell."

General Meaning.

The three-eyed Siva, addressing Pārvati, said ; Oh
vine-like Pārvati ! If you would know, who will fall
into the depths of hell, it is he, whose nature it is to
labor with seductive words to possess himself of another's
property, or another's wife

Now reflect, that this is a criterion fixed by Siva
himself. It is as though he pronounced judgment upon
himself, and upon Vishnu. For was it not Vishnu,

who feloniously appropriated the property of others? And was it not Siva, who, going to Tārugāvana, and singing voluptuous songs in the streets, bewitched the wives of the Rishis and corrupted their chastity? Hence, according to the criterion established by Siva himself; he, far from being a god, is only a hell-deserving sinner. Yet you affirm, that this Siva, the destroyer of female chastity, is the Sovereign Destroyer of all worlds. Does not this also sound like a piece of drollery?

Brethren! We do not say these things in the way of abuse. There is not such a thought in our heart. But remember that there is falsehood in the world as well as truth. Now it is plainly our duty, not only to establish the true, but also to overthrow the false. When we speak as we have of your Triad, we do not invent anything anew. We exhibit only what is related in your own Sastras. Remember the proverb,

"Truth told irritates the blear-eyed,"

and be not displeased with us. If you take umbrage at all, take it at your Sastras. For is it not they, which declare that your gods lied, stole, murdered, and committed other like crimes? The most reasonable thing then for you to do is to pronounce such Sastras worthless, and getting angry not with us, but with them, tear and burn and reduce them to ashes, thus venting your wrath on its proper objects. All that we say, calculated to injure your feelings, is said only for your good. You yourselves have a saying, that,

"He whose speech provokes tears, speaks for your life; but he whose speech provokes laughter, speaks for your ruin."

Perhaps some of you will say, that the actions cited are nothing more than the "sports of deity." But is it not sheer nonsense to speak thus? Suppose some one, creeping into your house, should steal and carry off your milk, your butter and your curds; would you on discovering the theft say, "Ha! Ha! Very good, this is excellent sport; nothing could be more delightful?"

Suppose one came into your village, and, stealing into your household, bewitched and ravished your wives and your daughters; would you applauding exclaim, " Oh ! this is capital fun, and a most innocent diversion ?" Would you, laughing with pleasure, pronounce this also to be splendid sport ? No, you never could call such actions sport, but would at once and unqualifiedly condemn them as intolerable wickedness

Others of you will perhaps unthinkingly say, that the gods, being superior existences, are at liberty to do such things as these. But surely, this is as absurd a speech as the other. What ! is there a law, which forbids inferior beings to lie, steal, or commit adultery, and at the same time licenses superior beings to do those very things untrammelled ? Who established such a law ? If there is such a law, must we not think its maker an unprincipled villain ? A superior being is, as you well know, more intelligent than an inferior. If therefore he commits the same crime as an inferior, is he not the greater sinner of the two ? If a beggar steals, it is an offence. But if a king turns thief, is not his offence greater ? Moreover, is it not God, who gives us the true Sastra and teaches us the right way ? Now if He Himself, leaving that good way; walks in the way of wickedness; how can we at all affirm that he is God ?

CURAL: 84TH CHAPTER: 4TH STANZA.

Literal Translation.

" There is no greater fool in the world than he who, though he reads good books, apprehends their contents, and teaches them to others, does not himself walk in obedience to their precepts."

General Meaning.

In the whole world, there is no fool equal to him, who, though he reads excellent books, understands their contents, and communicates them to others, does not himself follow their teachings.

According to this respect of Tiruvalluvar your gods are fools. Although instructing others, they themselves have left the good way, and wandered about in all sorts of wicked paths ?*

But some say ; "If men do wrong, it is sin ; but if God does wrong, it is not sin." This also is quite absurd. Whoever the eater, Sugarcane is Sugarcane, and Margosa is Margosa. Whoever the doer, right is right, and wrong is wrong.

NALADIAR : 12TH CHAPTER : 2ND STANZA.

Literal Translation.

" Whoever the eater, sugar will not taste bitter ; Margosa, though the gods eat it, will taste bitter : So good and bad persons never at any time lose their peculiar natures."

General Meaning.

The good never lose their good dispositions, the wicked never lose their wicked dispositions. Be the eaters who they may, sugar will always be sweet ; but Margosa, though the celestials partake of it, will still be bitter.

In like manner, if the good God does wrong, it is sin and nothing but sin.

Oh People ! We have no heart to enlarge further upon the wicked deeds, and infamous conduct of Brahma, Vishnu, and Siva, whom you call gods. Which one of " the five great sins"† have they left uncommitted ? Which one of " the six evil dispositions," viz : lust, anger, avarice, sensuality, pride, and envy, have they not exhibited ?

This being so, it is as clear " as the Nelli fruit in one's hand," that they are not gods.

What good can we possibly derive from such persons as these, filled to overflowing as they are with sin, hatred, and revenge ? No good indeed ; but evil and only evil.

* For Illustrations, see Appendix page 81.

† The " five great sins" are murder, lust, theft, drunkenness, and falsehood.

NALADIAR : 13TH CHAPTER : 6TH VERSE.

Literal Translation.

" Thinking certain persons great, thou reliedst upon them.
But what will it be like, Oh thou who hast thus relied upon
them ! if thou shouldst discover, that there is really no greatness in those, on whom thou hast relied ? Listen. It will be
as if one, saying, ' There is sandal-paste in this box,'
should, on opening it, discover in it a snake."

Mark well the meaning of this stanza. Depending
upon a wicked person, in the confidence that he is
good, is as if one, believing a box to contain sandal-
paste, should, on opening it, find not sandal-paste, but
a venomous life-destroying serpent. Just so, if you
worship the Triad, believing them to be gods ; you will
be fatally deceived, and, far from gaining heaven, will
surely fall into hell. Renounce them therefore utterly,
and with them all the homage, which you have hitherto
been accustomed to render them.

Listen, Oh People ! If one blind man walks holding
by the shoulder of another blind man, neither of them
will reach the village ; but both will together tumble
into the ditch. In like manner, if we, who are sinners,
cling to the Triad, who are equally sinners ; it is certain,
that we, together with them, will fall into hell.
Therefore forsake them at once and for ever.

VAKKUNDAM : 9.

Literal Translation.

" Seeing evil men is evil ; hearing the words of graceless
evil men is evil ; telling the evil qualities of evil men is
evil ; associating with evil men is evil."

Oh People ! Is it not needful for us to inquire, who
the true God is ? Hear what one of your poets says :

Literal Translation.

" Oh Thou All-Pervading God ! What profit is it to
those, who know not Thee, though they master all science ?
What profit, though they acquire all manner of wealth ?
Will they gain heaven ?"

General Meaning.

Oh God! Acquire whatever science they may; accumulate whatever property they may; will those prosper, who know not Thee?

CURAL : 1ST CHAPTER ; 2ND STANZA.

Literal Translation.

" What profit accrues to those, who have mastered all learning, if they worship not the excellent feet of Him, who is possessor of pure knowledge ?"

General Meaning.

However much learning men may acquire; it is all useless, if they worship not the celestial feet of the pure and All-wise God.

ANONYMOUS STANZA.

Literal Translation.

" That is God, which exists, eternal and uncaused, in the duration, that has neither beginning nor end."

If now you ask, " Who is that God, who, without beginning or end, is the eternal First Cause ?" it is He, who is revealed in the Holy Veda of the Christians' faith. He is the Supreme Soul, who formless pervades all space. He is the Omniscient and Omnipotent one. He is the Immaculate Holy one. He is the inflexibly just one. He is the good and grace-abounding one. He is the perfectly truthful one. He is the eternal, infinite, and unchangeable one. He it is, who is the Author of the Universe. He it is, who created heaven and earth, with all things, that are in them. He it is, who framed our souls and our bodies. He it is, who sees all things, upholds all things, governs all things. The government He exercises is a government of love, of goodness, and of justice.

Hear now how we may attain to a knowledge of Him. It is a vain imagination to suppose, that we can know God by erecting an idol. Even if it were possible to obtain in the world an image resembling God, what would we gain by gazing upon it? Do a man's affairs become known to us by looking at his form? However intently we may gaze upon that form, we can thereby learn nothing whatever of his birth-place, or of his occupations, or of his good and evil dispositions, or of the comforts and discomforts he experiences, or of the honors and dishonors put upon him. But if that man should write out, from beginning to end, all these details concerning himself in a book, and send that book to us; we should at once become acquainted with him and his affairs, even though we had never at any time laid eyes on his form. In like manner, we can gain no knowledge whatever of God by means of images. But if God Himself graciously reveals to us, in a Sastra, the things, which we need to know concerning Him; we may, through that Sastra, learn to know him truly.

But again; it is the merest folly even to speak of any image, as being a resemblance of Deity. No one can, by any possibility, see God with his bodily eyes. This being so, who can frame an image, which shall be like Him? By what power of imagination can any man conceive, or by what skill of art can he devise, a form resembling the divine substance, which he has never beheld? Many and various are the images, which you have set up. But which one of them all will you venture to affirm resembles God? With a view of worshipping it, you have erected the image of Pillaiyār upon the bund of every tank, and upon the boundary of every village. To that Pillaiyār, you yourselves have given the name of Lambōdaran. The meaning of Lambōdaran, as you well know, is "the big-bellied." Now, though you should gaze ever so long upon his belly swelling out like a washerman's pot, and upon his elephant-face, and upon his broken tusk, and upon his depending trunk; what knowledge, we ask, would you thereby gain concerning God? Is God such as that? Far from acquiring any true knowledge of God from such an image; the more you gaze upon it, the falser will be the ideas you form about Him.

But furthermore ; God is without form.* How then is it possible to represent by a form Him, who is formless ? Is any one capable of contriving an image resembling the soul, which resides in our bodies ? Will any man venture to make a representation of the wind, which sweeps through the sky ? If not, how then will he set about framing an image of the formless invisible God, who created the soul, the wind, and all other substances ?

But some say, " Unless God Himself comes and speaks, visibly standing before us, we can know nothing about Him." This also is a senseless speech. The Queen governs this country. Yet she never comes and stands before us. Her commands go forth, and speed from town to town, and from village to village, throughout the whole land, and every one submits to those commands. We have never beheld the Queen ; yet by the laws which she publishes, and by the government which she exercises, and by the books which describe her qualities and her actions, we learn both what sort of a person she is, and what kind of deeds she performs. Just so, there is no need of God's coming and standing visibly before us. He has given us a Sastra, the Holy Bible. It has gone forth, and been published in every land. From that Sastra, all may gain a sure knowledge of His true nature and attributes.

Know then, that it is impossible to see God with our bodily eyes. As one of your poet's puts it :

" God may appear to the inner spiritual eye ; but to the eye of the flesh He is ever the invisible."

Know further, that it is equally impossible for a soul, while wandering in sinful ways, to see God. We find in one of your works the following address to God :

" Oh Thou Spirit of Wisdom ! who art invisible to those, in whose hearts flourish desires after this vain false world."

If then we wish to know God, the relinquishment of all sinful practices is an indispensable necessity.

* See a Sloka in the Appendix ; page 82.

As the eye and light are both necessary to our seeing objects in the natural world, so a corresponding eye and light are necessary to our gaining a knowledge of God. The pious heart is that eye. The true Sastra is that light. Hence if you read and believe and walk according to the Christian Veda with a reverent heart; you will know God, and your souls will be filled with rejoicing.

If you ask, " But what shall those do, who know not how to read ?" We reply ; let them study and learn as soon as possible to peruse that Sastra And if this also is impracticable, they can at least learn by the hearing of the ear.

CURAL : 42ND CHAPTER : 4TH STANZA.

Literal Translation.

" Though one be destitute of learning, let him listen while the learned read. The knowledge (he thus gains) will prove a staff to support him in adversity."

General Meaning.

Although a man cannot himself read, let him listen while others read. The knowledge he thus acquires will be to him a supporting staff. He who, though himself untaught, takes in, by the ear, the substance of the true Veda, and believes and walks according to it, becomes possessed, as it were, of a new eye. His listening ear is itself that eye.

Brethren ! we all need to know the true God, and to gain his favor. Otherwise we shall certainly fall into hell, and there endure everlasting torments. Our sins are the obstacle to our obtaining God's favor. He is the Holy One ; we are sinners. How shall we, who are sinners, gain access to Him, who is infinitely holy ? Who can answer this question ? The Christian Veda alone gives a satisfactory reply. The Holy Bible teaches us, that Jesus Christ came into the world to remove the sins, which prevent us from coming to God. God, the sovereign Lord of all grace, has taken pity upon man. He has sent His Son, Jesus Christ, to be our Saviour. That Lord Jesus is the only divine Guru. He alone is the true sin-destroyer. He came into the world, was born as a man, and lived here thirty three years. He lived a life of holiness. He revealed true doctrine. He shewed mercy upon all. He performed great wonders and miracles. He gave unmistakeable proofs, that He is the true God, and the divine Guru. He acquired merit for the world immersed in guilt. To open a way of expiation for sin, He offered up His own life as a sacrifice. To this end, He was fixed with nails to the cross. He was buried in the grave. On the third day, He rose thence alive with majesty. He commanded His disciples to go the world over, and preach to all nations the way of salvation from sin. Finally leaving the world, He ascended up to heaven, where He now reigns, the Sovereign Lord of all worlds.

If now you ask why He thus came into the world and was born, and lived, and acted, and taught, and died, and rose again, and ascended to heaven; know that it was for us. It was to expiate your sin and our sin, that He did all these things. He and He alone is the remover of the obstacle sin. If you believe on Him, and follow His teachings, your sins will all be taken away by Him, and by Him you will gain access to God. Then God will become your heavenly Father, regard you with infinite favor, and accept you as His children. Thus you will attain to the eternal bliss of heaven.

Who can refrain from acknowledging and adoring this gracious, loving God; who formed us in our mother's womb, who has protected and supported us until now, and who gave His own Son as a Savior to remove our sins, in order that He might thus restore us to Himself and to heaven?

APPENDIX TO NO. V.

ILLUSTRATIONS AND EXAMPLES.

(1.) Concerning the question, as to which one of the Hindu Triad is the greatest?

You say, that there are three gods, named respectively Brahma, Vishnu, and Siva. But you at the same time, admit, that there is one God, who is supreme and above all others. Hence, it becomes necessary to inquire and determine which one of the above-mentioned three is the greatest.

Let us begin with Brahma. Is he the greatest of the three ? Listen to your Sastra, telling you how Brahma told a lie, and how, on account of that lie, a curse was put upon him to the effect, that thenceforward none should do him homage.

ARUNAJALA PURANA : TIRUMALAI SARUKAM.

Literal Translation.

" Hear, Oh Vishnu ! the result of my coming. Brahma said, ' Traversing, in a moment, leagues an hundred thousand, I saw the head of Siva, the Supreme, and have returned ?' The flower of the wild-pine also said, ' It is true.' "

General Meaning.

When Brahma said, " Having seen Siva's head, I have returned ;" the wild-pine flower also bore witness saying, " It is true."

Literal Translation.

" Siva, seeing the piety of Vishnu, whose soul was melting with desire, graciously bestowed upon him many gifts. Then, (turning to Brahma) he cursed him saying, ' Oh Brahma, who dwellest ·in the beautiful perfume-breathing lotus ! Let there (henceforth) be upon earth no temple, and no worship to thee, (who hast told this lie.)' "

General Meaning.

Siva, after bestowing upon Vishnu many gifts, cursed Brahma, saying, " Henceforth let no temple be built, and no worship be offered to thee."

Observe now, that it is your own Sastra, which here declares it to be wrong for any to worship this Brahma, because, when he had failed to discover Siva's head, he lied saying, that he had seen it. Consequently Brahma cannot be the greatest.

If now we proceed to inquire, which one of the remaining two, viz., Vishnu and Siva, is the greatest; we are at once met by a tremendous outcry from all the Saiva Puranas, exclaiming with one voice, " Siva, Siva, and not Vishnu, is the greatest." For example :

SKANDA PURANA : DAKSHA KANDAM : DADHEECHI PADALA.

Literal Translation.

" Who, of old time, graciously caused Vishnu, and Brahma, and all the other gods to dwell in the boundless prosperity, which they still enjoy ? Who is the Immaculate one ? Who is he, who, himself without cause, is the First-cause of all the others ? Who, among all the gods, is it, but our Siva, who benignly dwelt in the shade of the stone-banyan ?"

General Meaning.

Among the gods, Siva is supreme. This verse affirms that Siva is the one Supreme God, and that he is the primaeval cause of Brahma, and Vishnu, and all the other gods.

But the moment we begin, on the other hand, to inquire of the Vaishnuva Puranas, they all, in their turn, assail us with deafening shouts, exclaiming, " Vishnu, Vishnu, and not Siva, is the greatest." For example:

B'HAGAVATA :

SRUTI GITTAI URAITTA AD'HYAYA.

Literal Translation.

" Oh holy Vishnu ! Oh Eternal, All-wise, and Ever-blessed God, who, thyself without beginning or end, art the alone cause of all things ! Oh Incomprehensible Source of Light ! We know no way of describing thy greatness other than by saying, that, besides thee, no substance whatever is the Supreme Brahm."

General Meaning.

Vishnu, and no other, is supreme.   In this stanza we are told, that Vishnu alone is the supreme deity, and that he is the first-cause of all the other gods.

Now, when we see your Sastras thus quarrelling with each other, we can find no ground for thinking, that they came from God; but are forced to the conclusion, that they are mere fables, concocted by the subtlety of men.

Again, your Sastras inform us, that, on some occasions, Vishnu vanquished Siva; and that, on other occasions, Siva vanquished Vishnu.   Reflect upon these conflicting statements, and say, whether they do not compel the belief, that neither of the two is greater than the other.   Moreover all this talk about their relative superiority and inferiority sounds very much like the history of quarrelsome men.   There is nothing of the divine in it.

(2.)   A Sanscrit Sloka affirming, that all who worship Siva are destined to eternal hell.

Literal Translation.

" All votaries of Siva, and all who follow (the teachings of) such votaries, are heretics and enemies to good Sastras. All who wish to gain heaven, separating themselves from the frightful-shaped retinue of Siva, and becoming devoid of impatience, attach themselves to the tranquil adherents of Vishnu."

General Meaning.

The devotees of Siva and the adherents of all such devotees are apostates, who have rejected the heaven-giving Sastras.   Therefore, all who wish to gain heaven renounce the service of the hideous Rudra, and worship the placid Vishnu.

(3.)   A Sanscrit Sloka affirming, that all, who worship Vishnu, are destined to eternal hell.

Literal Translation.

" The mere beholding of Vishnu is treason against Siva. By committing treason against Siva, men fall into dreadful hell. Of this there is no doubt. Hence it is never right even to mention the name of Vishnu."

General Meaning.

The very sight of Vishnu is treason against Siva. The result of such treason is hell. Therefore it is un-lawful even to pronounce the name of Vishnu.

(4.) Example affirming, that Vishnu created Brahma; and sitting upon a mortar stole curdled milk.

B'HAGAVATA : KADAVUL VALTTU.

Literal Translation.

"Hail beauteous Lotus, birth-place of the eight-eyed Brahma, and navel of my father Krishna! who, incarnate as the son of Nanda, placed under himself a mortar, and sitting thereon stole curdled milk from the roof-rope of the cowherds."

General Meaning.

Hail Lotus, which art the navel of the thief Krishna, and birth-place of Brahma!

(5.) Concerning those, who point out the good way to others; but fail to follow it themselves.

NEETINERI VILAKKAM.

Literal Translation.

"The empty words of those, who though they read and teach good books to others do not themselves follow the precepts they inculcate, have but one efficacy, which is this. They force on the part of their utterers the invention of excuses, calculated to silence those, who sneeringly ask; "How happens it, that you, who teach others, do not yourselves walk as you teach?"

General Meaning.

He, who would teach others, must himself walk according to his own teaching.

(6.) Sanscrit Sloka shewing, that the gods, who point out the path of purity, may not themselves do evil.

Literal Translation.

"The gods are those, who point out the path of purity; they will not follow an impure way."

General Meaning.

As the gods are teachers of purity, they will not themselves indulge in impurity.

(7.) Sanscrit Sloka shewing, that God is able to accomplish all things without hands, feet, eyes and other such members.

Literal Translation.

"He has neither hand nor foot, yet he seizes and moves with celerity. He has no eye, yet he sees. He has no ear, yet he hears. He knows what he needs to know. There is none, who knows him. They call him, The Soul, The First cause, The glorious."

General Meaning.

They call him God, who moves and seizes without hands and feet, who sees without eyes, who hears without ears, who knows all that is fit to be known, and who is himself known by none.

(8.) Concerning the worship of Garuda, the vehicle of the butter-stealing Vishnu.

B'HAGAVATA: KADAVUL VALTTU.

Literal Translation.

" All hail to the two feet of Garuda, king of birds ! whose hand upholds the comely foot of Vishnu ; who stealing butter ate it, and who, in order that the blemish of discord might cease from the earth, slew the Asura named Mura."

General Meaning.

All hail to the divine feet of Garuda !

SCRIPTURE TEXTS.

(1.) There is but one God.
   Isaiah 44. 6, 7.   Mark 12. 29, 32.
   Isaiah 45. 5, 6, 18, 22.   1 Cor. 8. 4.
(2.) He is without form.
   John 4. 24.   1 Tim. 1. 17.
(3.) He is Omnipresent.
   Psalm 139. 1 to 12.   Jer. 23. 23, 24.

(4.) He is Omniscient.
 1 Cor. 28. 9. Rom. 11. 33, 34. Heb. 4. 13.
(5.) He is Omnipotent.
 Job 42. 2. Jer. 32. 17. Rev. 1. 8.
(6.) He is infinitely Just.
 Psalm 119. 137, 138, 142. Zeph. 3. 5.
(7.) He is infinitely Holy.
 Isaiah 6. 3. Heb. 1. 13. Rev. 15. 4.
(8.) He is infinitely Merciful.
 Exodus 34. 6. Joel 2. 13.
 Psalm 103. 8, 9, 10. Luke 6. 35, 36.
(9.) He is infinitely Truthful.
 Deut. 32. 4. Num. 23. 19.
(10.) He is without beginning and end.
 Psalm 90. 2. 1 Tim. 1. 17. Rev. 1. 8.
(11.) He is Unchangeable.
 Mal. 3. 6. Heb. 13. 8. James 1. 17.
(12.) He is the Creator and Upholder of all.
 Gen. 1. 1. Heb. 11. 3. Neh. 9. 6.
(13.) The Bible is necessary to a true knowledge of
Him.
 1 Cor. 1. 21. Mat. 11. 27.
 Rom. 10. 14 to 18. 2 Tim. 3. 16, 17.
(14.) No images of God to be set up.
 Exod. 20. 4, 5, 6. Lev. 26. 1. Deut. 27. 15
(15.) The holy alone shall see God.
 Mat. 5. 8.

ADDRESS No. VI.

~~~~~~~~

EXPIATION.

OH People! That sin must be expiated; and that, if it is not expiated, the sinner cannot enter heaven, but will surely fall into hell, are unquestionable truths well known and freely admitted by all. But with regard to the means of effecting such expiation, men have doubted much; and, becoming greatly bewildered in mind, have invented ways of bringing it about, as numerous as they are worthless. Now it is plain, that if we adopt a false method of expiation, blindly believing it to be a true one, we shall gain nothing thereby; but, on the contrary, only involve ourselves in greater sin and guilt and ruin. Hence the need of careful discrimination. Worthless ways must, on the one hand, be rejected; and, on the other, the true way must be sought after, ascertained, and resolutely adopted.

SOME AMONG YOU AFFIRM THAT IN ORDER TO EXPIATE SIN IT IS NECESSARY TO MAKE PILGRIMAGES AND VISIT SACRED PLACES.

In accordance with this affirmation, numbers of people, gathering in vast crowds, go to Cāsi, to Conjeveram, to Tripaty, to Rāmēsuram, and to many other places. But among all these multitudes, there is not, we are sorry to say one person who ever stops to think or to inquire, whether the pilgrimage he undertakes is right or wrong, profitable or worthless.

Oh People! why do you go to these places? Does not God, who dwells there, dwell here also? Can it be possible, that the all-pervading Deity is wanting only in those localities, where you happen to live? What strange, incongruous talk is this? When God is as certainly present in your village, as He is present in all other places ; what means this running to and fro, and wandering hither and thither, as if He were to be sought and found only in some particular situation ? Surely your thus roaming from town to town in search of the Deity, who is always present in your own village, is as insane a proceeding as that of a man "seeking fire with a lighted lamp in his hand."*

Hear what one of your poets says :

TAYUMANAVAR.

Translation.

" Oh God ! The Veda tells us, that Thou art equally present everywhere. Is it then right for us, without seeking Thee where we are, to wander hither and thither in search of Thee ?"

Oh People ! Why do you go to those places ? Is your nature changed by going there ? Does the thief, who goes to Cāsi, become honest, when he sees that town ? Does the passionate man, who visits Conjeveram, become, by beholding it, gentle and kind ? Is the liar, who reaches Rāmēsuram, transformed into a true man ? Is the villain, who climbs the Tripaty hill, changed into a good person ? Nothing of all this. Though one should go and visit every sacred place in the wide world, his old bad disposition would not be thereby changed, nor would he thereby acquire a new good disposition.†

Hear the testimony of Sivavākkiar.

SIVAVAKKIAR.

Translation.

" Crying Casi ! Casi ! you run, oh People ! until your legs ache with weariness. But however much you run to Casi, and bathe in the river there ; will black ever become white ?"

---

* See Appendix : page 95.

† See Appendix : page 96.

Oh People! why do you go to those places? Do you go expecting that any profit will thereby accrue to you?* If so your expectations are met in a very peculiar way. A strange sort of profit it is you get surely enough! Your bodies become weary and worn and thin. Your clothes wear out. Your feet, pricked with thorns, and chafed on rough stones, become sore and painful. The money you take with you is wasted and lost. The dust and dirt of many lands cover your persons. Strange diseases, and unknown distempers seize upon your systems. It may be, that you fall among robbers. It may be, that you become utterly ruined and destroyed. These profits are, we allow, certain to accrue to you.† But why need you go to distant places in search of such gains? If you really wish for them, surely you may, with much less difficulty, get them in your own villages. You know the common saying,

"A sore foot was all he got for his pains."

Oh People! what good is there in thus vainly roaming and wandering about, like a straw tossed hither and thither upon the waves of the sea? To suppose that sin can be removed by making pilgrimages to sacred places is the uttermost folly. Holy places you call them indeed; but to designate them aright, you should call them all unholy places. How is it, for example, when great festivals are held in them? Do not multitudes of villains, and debauchees and thieves, and black-legs gather together there in crowds? Do not thousands of harlots throng their streets? Are not all kinds of uncleanness, and vice, and debauchery freely practised in them? We are utterly at a loss to understand by what casuistry you call such places as these holy. The truth is, that they are places fitted to produce nothing except luxuriant harvests of sin. It stands therefore to reason, that they should be called

* See Appendix: page 96.

† See Appendix: page 96.

unholy. By going to such places, your sin, far from diminishing, is sure to be increased an hundred-fold. It is as if one, having gone to bathe, should plaster himself all over with mud.

OTHERS AMONG YOU AFFIRM, THAT BATHING IN SACRED WATERS IS THE SUREST MEANS OF EXPIATING SIN.

You sound the praises of the Ganges, the Jumna, the Kavery and other rivers. You declare that their waters are holy, and that every thing, which touches them, is sure of entering the world of the gods. But on what grounds are we to assent to all this talk ? Thousands of crows descending bathe every day, with fluttering wings, in those sacred streams. Vast herds of buffalos, immersing their entire bodies with the exception only of the nose, bathe daily in those holy waters. Swarms of water-flies, playing with unceasing motion upon the shining surface, bathe continually in those consecrated floods. Multitudes of fish and frogs, which are born, and grow, and live in those rivers, bathe evermore submerged in their heavenly depths. Now if it be true, as you say, that " every thing, which touches those sacred rivers, is sure to enter the world of the gods ;" how happens it, we ask, that not a single one of all the crows, or of all the buffalos, or of all the water-flies, or of all the fish, or of all the frogs, which unceasingly frequent their illustrious waters, has, up to this time, ever attained to that blissful abode ? Nay more ; how is it, that the fish, which plays continually within the very bosom of those sacred streams, has failed, not only to get to heaven, but even to get rid of its offensive smell ?

PAMBATTI SITTAR PADAL.

Translation.

" Though you wash a stinking fish many times every day with pure water, will its bad odor be thereby removed ? Never. Know, Oh my Soul ! that, in like manner, the filth acquired by the body can never be removed by bathing in many rivers."

Again: we are told, that if men touch those sacred waters, all their sins will at once be removed. This also is a great falsehood. It is not the soul, but the body only, which comes in contact with water. Now sin originates not in the body, but in the soul. Can the water reach to the soul, and cleanse it? What connection can there be between the soul and water, which are substances foreign the one to the other?

AGAPPEY SITTAR PADAL.

Translation.

"Though you bathe in sacred rivers, Oh Agappēy! sin will not be taken away. Though filth of body be thereby removed, Oh Agappēy! the soul's guilt will still remain. Would you know, Oh Agappēy! the way of expiating sin? Oh Agappēy! The knowledge of God, and the attainment of inward purity are the only sacred rivers, which can wash it away."

Oh People! If you go down into those rivers, and bathe rubbing yourselves thoroughly; it may be, that the dirt, which adheres to your bodies, will be removed. But even this is doubtful. If you ask why, listen and we will tell you. Those rivers, having become famous, multitudes of people resort to them. Many enter them with fetid bodies. Many go down into them with unclean diseases. Many bathe in them with foul ulcers, incurable wounds, and running sores. Yet, notwithstanding all this, you descend into those same rivers polluted with the filth and fetor of these infected crowds, proclaiming as you go, that their waters are pure and holy. It certainly looks very doubtful whether even the dirt upon your bodies will be thereby removed. Better a thousand times for you to wash in the water of your own wells and tanks, than to go and bathe in such rivers as these.

Oh People! Bathe in what water you may, your sins will not thereby be removed. So some of your own sages also have declared. For example;

Translation.

"You bathe, Oh Men! in sacred rivers. You read like proficients the Sastras, which discourse of prayer and worship. You wander about ceaselessly roaming from shrine to shrine, and bathing in river after river. If any ask why you do all this? you in reply, citing for authority Sastras made up of false and distorted fabrications, declare, that you expect thereby to change your nature, and attain to a higher birth. Would you learn, Oh Blockheads! what you are? You are weak simpletons, unacquainted with the fitness of things. Know that after all your pains, you will be but brutes devoid of knowledge."

Remember also the saying;

"A crow cannot become a swan, though it bathe in the Ganges."*

SOME THINK, THAT SIN CAN BE EXPIATED BY BRAHMINS.

The Brahmin, regardless of the wise saying,

"Be not ruined by arrogance,"

dares to call himself god. Your Sastra also affirms the same thing.

NALLA PILLAI BARATA, SANTI PARUVAM: VIDUMANAI KANDA SARUKAM.

Literal Translation.

"If a good and equitable king, estimating Brahmins to be superior beings in comparison with Siva, Vishnu, Brahma and the other gods, shews affection towards them, he will be faultless. His merit will accumulate with a long life. No calamity will befal the subjects of his kingdom. The seven clouds will rain upon his land. Sacrifices will abound."

General Meaning.

This verse tells us, that the king, who shows kindness to Brahmins, regarding them as greater than Brahma, Vishnu, Siva, and all the other gods, is the most immaculate of princes. He will be blessed with long life, and an accumulation of merit. His subjects

* See Appendix, page 97.

will be prosperous, and free from all calamity; and his land will be favored with abundance of rain.*

Now why does the Brahmin thus boast himself to be God? Know you not his design? He does it simply in order that he may exalt himself, abase all others, heap up money, and fill his belly. The wonder of wonders is, not that he ventures thus to boast himself divine; but that you blindly admitting his blasphemous claims, worship him, and believe that sin can, by him, be expiated. If the Brahmin is really god, all things belong to him. How is it then, that he works for wages in the Cutchery? If the Brahmin is really god, he can give and preserve life as well as destroy it. How is it then, that, when his child dies, he weeps and beats his breast in sorrow? If the Brahmin is really god, he is possessed of all wisdom. Whence then the common saying,

     " A Brahmin's wit is ever behind hand?"

These things being so, need we tell you, that all this talk of the Brahmin about his being himself a god is the merest gasconade? And when your Sastra insanely calls the Brahmin divine, is it not the best of proof that your Sastra is false? The Brahmin is no god. He is, just like all the rest of us, a weak and sinful man. The Brahmin, on account of his arrogance, and the innumerable other sins which he has committed, is ready to fall into hell. Tell us then, we pray you, how in the name of reason your sins can be expiated by him?†

SOME AFFIRM, THAT SIN CAN BE EXPIATED BY DWELL-ING IN DESERTS, AND BY WANDERING AS ASCETICS.

Now if, on the one hand, you say that going and dwelling as hermits in a desert is the best way of expiating sin; it follows as a matter of course, that since all men need such expiation, all should without delay go into the wilderness and live there. But do

* See a Sloka in the Appendix: page 97.

† See Appendix, page 97.

you not see, that the moment they do so your desert becomes a town overflowing with inhabitants? Besides, all this vaunted going into desert places, all this growing of the hair, the beard and the nails, and all this devouring of wild fruits, flowers, dried leaves and roots, is conduct more befitting a brute than a man. How then can your sins be thereby expiated?*

If, on the other hand, you say that wandering about as a Sanniyāsi is the best way of expiating sin, you are as wide as ever of your mark. For how in reason can anyone's sin be expiated by his leaving house and home, and wandering from country to country, staff and potsherd in hand, as a begging vagrant? If you will only observe the conduct of the Sanniyāsis, who roam from village to village in your land; you will be at once convinced, that sin, far from being removed, is greatly increased by their pretended asceticism. These Sanniyāsis get angry, and utter the vilest abuse. They curse and swear immoderately. They sing lewd songs. They ruin women. They steal. No uncleanness is too filthy for them to wallow in. What! Is this the way of expiation? Is this the path to heaven? Are not you aware, that none but idle vagabonds assume this disguise of asceticism? Too lazy to work themselves, they wander about as Sanniyāsis, that they may make a living out of others' toil.†

These things being so, it is plain, that neither dwelling in deserts, nor roaming as Sanniyāsis is the way of expiating sin. Such means of expiation, far from being appointed by God, are but the false and worthless devices of designing men.

The people of this land have invented yet many other ways of expiation. They delude themselves with the belief, that sin can be removed by placing lights in temples, by putting on the Vib'huti and the Nāmam,‡

* See Appendix: page 98.

† See Appendix: page 98.

‡ The Vibhuti and Nāmam are the sacred marks worn on the forehead by the Sivites and Vishnuvites.

by carrying the Kāvadi,* by wearing the Harikanda,†
by rolling their bodies in the dust around a temple;
by treading on fire, by shaving the head, by practising
various austerities, and by giving alms and presents.
Now, all these put together cannot remove a single sin.
Trusting to reach heaven by any of them will end as
disastrously as would the attempt of a man to cross a
flooded river by catching hold of a puppy's tail, under
the delusion, that he would thereby reach the opposite
shore.   Both the puppy and the dolt clinging to its
tail would be swept away by the current, and perish
miserably together.

Oh People ! All men have broken the laws of God,
and sinned greatly against Him.   God is a holy and
just being, and therefore both hates and punishes all
sin.   The punishment which He inflicts is eternal hell.
Since you have committed sin, you are exposed to the
wrath of God, and to the torments of hell.   Perform
what deeds, and practise what austerities you may ;
think you, that you can thereby either assuage His
wrath, or escape the penalty He has decreed ?   Never,
it is an impossibility.

NALADIAR : 17TH CHAPTER : 4TH STANZA.

Literal Translation.

" The richly tinted Cobra-de-capella, though hidden
securely in a mountain-cleft, quakes at the angry roar of
thunder rolling in the distant sky. So when the great
become angry, their enemies cannot escape, though they
may have taken refuge in an impregnable fortress."

General Meaning.

The Cobra-de-capella, though hidden in his den,
trembles at the sound of distant thunder. So when the
great are angry, their foes cannot survive, though they
deem themselves perfectly secure.

* The Kāvadi is the sacred pole carried on the shoulders by religious
mendicants to gather offerings for the service of the temples.

† The Harikanda is an iron grate, worn on the neck by devotees
as a means of self-torture.

Mark well the import of this verse. A serpent, thinking to escape the thunderbolt, crawls into its den; but even there the lightning strikes its head and kills it. In like manner, you, thinking to escape from God's wrath against sin, make pilgrimages to sacred places, bathe in holy rivers, and perform many other similar deeds. You imagine, that these deeds are for you an impregnable fort, within which you are safe from the punishment of hell. But remember, that the God who is angry with you is a God of infinite justice, and of almighty power. Will your poor deeds prove, think you, a sure defence against His wrath? Will they rescue you from your danger? Never.

" If the ocean boils, where will you get water for cooling."

Do you ask why God is angry with us? It is only because of the sins, which we have committed. If then our sins are expiated, His wrath will not seize upon us, neither will it cast us into hell. If our sins are expiated, we will become the children of God, and will reach heaven, the place of his abode.

Brethren! The expiation of sin being a task wholly beyond our own power, it is of the utmost necessity, that we anxiously inquire, whether there is not some other way of effecting this great end? There is such a way. God is infinitely merciful. Therefore He has Himself made that way for us. He has sent His Son Jesus Christ into the world to save us. That Jesus Christ, moved by love to us, came to earth for the very purpose of opening a way of expiating our sins. Listen, while we explain to you who He is, and what the divine work He accomplished.

Jesus Christ, the Saviour of all men, is the Son of the Eternal God. He is the Sovereign Lord of all worlds. He is the Creator of the Universe. The Sun, the Moon, and the stars; Heaven, Earth and Hell were all framed, and are all supported by Him. He beheld all mankind pursuing the way to hell. His soul melted with pity at the sight. He left heaven, and coming down to earth, became incarnate as a man. His very name is fitted to bring hope and joy to our hearts. Jesus Christ! a name holy and exalted. The word Jesus means Saviour. The word Christ signifies the Guru who teaches truth, the Priest who makes atonement for sin, and the King who governs and preserves the world. He is the All-wise, the All-merciful, the Almighty, the Eternal God. He has no equal. There is neither likeness nor comparison, by which he may be described. The purpose of His coming down to earth was the expiation of our sins. He dwelt in this world thirty-three years. He lived as a man before the eyes of men, yet His life was a life of immaculate purity. He displayed His divine nature and His boundless grace. He performed numberless miracles. He drove away men's diseases with the power of His word. By a simple command, He cured blindness, deafness, dumbness, and other similar defects and maladies. His benevolence beamed forth everywhere, like light from the Sun. The sorrowful, seeking Him in crowds, gained joyful hearts and smiling faces. In the end, He endured great agonies and a most cruel death. Fixed to the cross with nails driven through His hands and His feet, He gave up His life. He was then buried within a tomb in the earth. On the third day, He rose out of it alive, and appeared in glory. Revealing Himself to His disciples, He commanded them to go into all the world, and to preach Him, and the way of expiation He had made, to every creature. Finally, in the presence of many witnesses, He left this earth, which He had redeemed by His blood, and rising through the air, and disappearing among the clouds, returned to heaven, from whence he came.

Perhaps you will ask why this Jesus Christ, the Lord of heaven, came down to earth, and suffered thus ? This is an excellent question. Listen attentively while we answer it. Jesus Christ came into this world and suffered in order that He might expiate our sins. It was because His love is a boundless love, that He consented to suffer thus for us. On account of our sins, we deserve to endure the eternal punishment of hell. To rescue us from that penalty, Jesus Christ bore it all in our stead upon earth. He, who was without sin, took our sins upon Himself, and atoned for them all. He also procured boundless merits for us. He alone is capable of doing meritorious deeds. It is only by the sufferings of Jesus Christ, and by the merits of Jesus Christ, that the way of expiation for sinners has been made. But for whom will these sufferings and these merits avail? Mark well the answer. For those and those only among men, who feel their sins, truly mourn that they have offended against the good God, leave off all wicked practices, and believe in Jesus Christ as their only Saviour. All such persons Jesus Christ will surely save. He will blot out their sins. He will send His Holy Spirit to cleanse and sanctify their souls. He will make them the children of God. Such persons will not fall into hell. They will live for ever blessed with Christ in heaven. But all those, who do not embrace Him as their Saviour, will as certainly be turned into hell, and there be immersed in eternal woe.

Beloved Friends! Believe on this Jesus Christ. The way He has opened is the only way. There is no other.

APPENDIX TO NO. VI.

ILLUSTRATIONS AND EXAMPLES.

(1.) Why do you go to those sacred places? Is God, who is there, not here also?

VEMANAR, 3 : 257.

Literal Translation.

"Hear, O Vēmana, beloved of the Lord! They go with great joy crying Casi, Casi. Is God, who is there, not here also? If the heart be right, He is both here and there."

General Meaning.

As God is eveywhere present, men need not visit Casi to find Him.

(2.) Why do you go to those places? Will your nature be thereby changed?

VEMANAR, 3 : 253.

Literal Translation.

"Hear, O Vĕmana, beloved of the Lord! A Mohammedan will not become a Vaishnuva by going to Tripaty. Neither will a harlot become a virtuous woman, though she visit Casi—If a dog go to the Godavery, will it be transformed into a lion?"

General Meaning.

One's nature is not changed by making pilgrimages to sacred places.

(3.) Why do you go to those places? Will you get any good thereby?

VEMANAR, 3 : 272.

Literal Translation.

"Hear, O Vĕmana, beloved of the Lord! Although a man with eager desire visits Casi, Madura, Conjeveram, Gaya, Prayāgayu, and Rāmésuram, he will not get true knowledge. The effort is vain and fruitless."

General Meaning.

Though one goes with longing desire and sees Casi, Madura, Conjeveram, and other sacred places, he gets no profit thereby.

(4.) Why do you go to those sacred places? You suffer many losses thereby.

VEMANAR, 3 : 271.

Literal Translation.

"O Vĕmana! The ignorant rabble, thinking that God is not present where they live, roam from shrine to shrine; and, having lost all the money they had in hand, return to their homes utterly ruined."

General Meaning.

Fools, who think that God is not present where they live, make sacred pilgrimages, foolishly waste their money, and come back ruined to their homes.

(5.) The heart is not cleansed by bathing in the Ganges.

SANSCRIT SLOKA.

Literal Translation.

" He who has guilt on his conscience will not become clean, though he wash himself, till he dies, with all the water of the Ganges, and (smear himself) with mountain-loads of mud."

General Meaning.

A bad man will never become a good man, though he smear himself with mountains of mud, and bathe in the Ganges until his dying day.

(6.) A lamentation about aching legs.

PATTANATTU PILLAI.

Literal Translation.

" I went as far as Casi, and got an aching leg. I climbed up jungly mountains, and got an aching leg."

General Meaning.

The only fruit of going to Casi and other such places is leg-weariness.

(7.) The Brahmin is God.

SANSCRIT SLOKA.

Literal Translation.

" All worlds are subject to God ; God is subject to the Mantra ; that Mantra is subject to the Brahmin ; the Brahmin is God to me."

General Meaning.

The Universe is dependent on God ; God is dependent on the Mantra ; the Mantra is dependent on the Brahmin ; therefore the Brahmin is my God.

(8.) The Brahmin, who abuses other men, will fall into hell.

VEMANAR, 3 : 223.

Literal Translation.

" Hear, O Vemana, beloved of the Lord ! There is no baser person upon earth than the villain, who abuses Sudras by calling them Sudras. When he dies, he will go to hell."

General Meaning.

There is no meaner person in the wide world than the man, who vilifies others by calling them Sudras. Such an one is doomed to hell.

(9.) Asceticism, or the renunciation of all earthly attachments, is the greatest good.

PATTANATTU PILLAI.

Literal Translation.

" Teeth unstained (by chewing Betel) ; garments of filthy cloth ; a soul patient and free from guile ; food unpalatable and nauseous ; an outer verandah or the bare ground for a bed ; a potsherd to receive alms and serve as a plate : these constitute perfect riches. So declare the great and precious Vedas for the information of the world."

General Meaning.

The Vedas declare, that the renunciation of all earthly attachments is the perfection of wealth.

(10.) Asceticism is useless.

VEMANAR, 3 : 179.

Literal Translation.

" Hear, O Vemana, beloved of the Lord ! What though one leaves home and family, wears an iron fore-lap, re-nounces all desire for food and drink, and lives a lonely recluse ; will heaven be gained thereby ?"

General Meaning.

It is useless for a man to leave his house and family, to wear an iron fore-lap, to rid himself of all desire for food, and to live alone as an ascetic. Heaven cannot be gained by such means as these.

SCRIPTURE TEXTS.

(1.) God will, in His justice, punish sin.
Psalm 7. 11. Psalm 9. 17. Psalm 11. 5, 6.
Rom. 1. 18. Rom. 2. 8, 9.

(2.) Men cannot save themselves by their good deeds.
Gal. 3. 10, 11, 12, 21.

(3.) Men cannot save themselves by sacrifices and offerings.
Micah 6. 6, 7. Heb. 10. 4. Isaiah 1. 11 to 18.

(4.) God sent His Son into the world to save sinners:
John 3. 16, 17. 1 John 4. 9, 14.

(5.) Jesus Christ bore our sins.
Isaiah 53. 4, 5, 6. 2 Cor. 5. 21. 1 Peter 2. 24.

(6.) He offered Himself a sacrifice and died to remove sin.
Heb. 9. 26. Titus 2. 14. 1 Peter 3. 18.

(7.) He rose again for our justification.
Romans 4. 25.

(8.) Those who believe on Him will be saved.
John 6. 40, 47. Acts 10. 45. Rom. 5. 1, 2.

(9.) Those who do not believe on Him cannot be saved.
John 3. 18, 36. Mark 16. 16.

ADDRESS No. VII.

~~~~~~~~~

MANTRAS.

THE people of this country have invented many and various kinds of Mantras. Foolishly believing that by repeating these Mantras sin is expiated, merit procured, and heaven gained, they neglect seeking the true way of salvation, and are thus for ever ruined.

These Mantras are carefully concealed as great secrets. They are never pronounced publicly, but are communicated only by whispering them secretly in the ears of learners. Now, if Mantras are really good and useful things, there ought to be no objection to teaching them in such a way, that all may learn and profit by them. If they are really the truth, what valid reason can there be for so carefully concealing them? Who is it that dreads the light of day, if it be not a thief? Are we not then right in concluding, that Mantras, which avoiding the light lurk always in darkness, are, like the thief, false and untrustworthy?

But Brahmins and others succeed in deluding many persons by the following excuse; namely, that the glory of the Mantra is so great as to preclude the possibility of its being openly revealed. Hence it becomes necessary for us to examine a little into the nature of these Mantras. We must inquire whether or no these Mantras are really possessed of the glory, which is thus attributed to them. A rogue, having made an ornament of brass, artfully exhibits it in the dark, and declares that it is gold. But he will not venture to bring it out in the light; for the moment he does so, every body will at once see that it is nothing but brass and of course worthless. In like manner, if the Mantras, which the Brahmins so studiously conceal, and so secretly communicate, can only be dragged out into the light, we shall readily arrive at a just estimate of their true nature and value.

FIRST.

They hold in the highest possible veneration the Pran'ava Mantra, which consists of the single syllable " Om." The Mánava Dharmma Sastra says, that burnt-offerings and sacrifices together with all other Vedic rites and ceremonies will be abolished; that while these must all pass away, the Mantra " Om" will never pass away, but endure for ever; that this Mantra is itself the Veda, and that it is itself God.* Furthermore, we find it stated in various other of your Sastras that the four Vedas sprung from the Mantra† " Om ;" that whoever pronounces it pronounces all the four Vedas; that the word " Om" is itself light to the soul, and that, by its own virtue, it confers heavenly bliss.

If all this be true, it is plain that no one need in future trouble himself about reading the Scriptures, or about worshipping God, or about leading a religious life. The syllable " Om" alone being all-sufficient, every thing else is, as a matter of course, superfluous and therefore useless. Oh People ! why do you believe such stuff as this ? Is it not the sheerest folly to suppose, that, after renouncing the God who created us, and openly violating His laws, we can obtain heaven by simply uttering the syllable " Om ?" We have committed many sins against God. Judge now for yourselves whether the doctrine, which teaches, that all those sins will be at once removed by pronouncing the word " Om," is a doctrine from God, or whether it is a mere device invented by wicked men ? If men believe, that sin is taken away by merely uttering the monosyllable " Om ;" who among them all will fear to sin ? The whole world would at once become immersed in wickedness.

* See Appendix : page 115.

† See Appendix : page 115.

But further ; let us inquire what is the substance and meaning of this Mantra "Om."

KANJI PURANA : KUMARA KOTTA PADALA.

Literal Translation.

"The word Om is placed at the beginning of all Sastras (as their cause.) Sages tell us, that this word means the three, viz., Brahma, Vishnu and Siva. It is the mystic essence of the entire Vedas. It is spiritual light. It is full of the excellence, which dwells in the souls of Yogis. Those only who know this Pranava can attain to heaven."

General Meaning.

This stanza tells us, that the meaning of the word "Om" is Brahma, Vishnu and Siva.

Let us enter a little into the details of its substance. We are told, that the syllable "Om" consists of three members. These are A, U, and M. A and U united become O. O and M being joined, we have "Om." A. indicates Vishnu. U. indicates Siva. M. indicates Brahma. The three letters conjoined in the word "Om" point out the Hindu Triad. Hence this "Om" is a Mantra which, both as to its origin and its object, refers solely to that Triad. But what, on inquiry, do we learn about the nature and conduct of the persons composing that Triad ? Does not the Arunājala Purāna tell us, that Brahma told a lie ? Does not the B'hāgavata inform us that Vishnu stole ? Does not the Skanda Purāna relate that Siva ravished the wives of the Rishis ? Surely we need not tell you that this Mantra, referring as it does to a Triad who lied, stole and committed adultery, can never remove our sins and save us ; but is, on the contrary, fitted only to corrupt and destroy by dragging us into the commission of the same and similar villanies.

SECOND.

They tell us, that the Gayatri Mantra is possessed of extraordinary virtue and power. Here is the Mantra.

|| Om ||

|| B'hūr—B'huvar—Svar ||*

|| Tat Savitur Varényam B'hargō Dévasya
D'hímahì D'hiyō Yōnaha Pratsōdayāt. ||

Literal Translation.

" Om—Earth—Air—Heaven—We meditate on the supreme splendour of the Sun, that god who governs our minds."

Brahmins repeat this every day without missing; but among them all there is not one in a thousand, who knows what it means. Parrot-like they simply mutter it with their lips. We give you its meaning here.

General Meaning of the Gayatri.

Om—Earth—Air—Heaven—We meditate on the supreme lustre of the Sun. He is the god, who governs and illumines our understanding.

Now hear what is said about this Mantra in the Mānava Dharmma Sāstra. If one recites it a thousand times within a month; he will become holy, ridding himself of his sins as a serpent rids itself of its slough.†
It matters not whether he does or does not do any thing else: let him but mutter this Gayatri, and it is enough. That alone will give him heaven. So says the abovementioned Sastra.‡

Consider well the scope and meaning of this Mantra, which they extol as so great. It is a Mantra addressed to the Sun. Its substance is as follows :—

" Oh Sun! We meditate on thy brightness. Direct thou us."

* The words " B'hūr-B'huvar-Svar," compose what is called the Vyāhruti Mantra ; but it is customary to repeat them in conjunction with the Gāyatri.

The word " Om" being analyzed becomes A. U. M. A. means Vishnu ; U. means Siva, and M. means Brahma. B'hūr is the Earth. B'huvar is the space between the earth and the Sun. Svar is the region occupied by the planets.

† See Appendix : page 116.

‡ See Appendix : page 116.

Is it right thus to call the Sun God, and worship it as such? Will any sane man venture to affirm, that the Sun is really God? We place lamps to give us light in our dwelling-houses. Those houses are but small, and, as is fit, the lights we place in them are also small. But the earth is a house large and spacious enough for all mankind to live in. Consequently it requires a proportionably large lamp. As men suspend hanging lamps from the ceilings in their houses, so God has suspended the Sun as a lamp in the firmament, which extends like a vast roof over the immense house of the earth. Hence the Sun is not God, but merely a large lamp for the lighting up of the world. We are bound to worship the God, who placed that lamp in the sky; but what shall we say of those, who deserting Him worship only the light which He has suspended there? Let us suppose a case by way of illustration. A poor man wishing to see and ask a favor of some prince goes to his house. On arriving there, he instead of seeking the prince's presence advances towards the hanging lamp, and bowing to it with clasped hands addresses it thus; "My Lord! I have sought your worshipful presence. I am a poor man, who would humbly ask of your lordship a favor. I pray your lordship will graciously grant me my petition." What in such a case would the household servants do? Would they not all running together exclaim; "What madman is this come here on a fool's errand? See, he takes the lamp for the master of the house. Who knows what such a maniac won't do next?" And so saying, would they not at once drive him out of the premises? The application is obvious. There is one only true God, the Creator not of one Sun, but of myriads of Suns and Moons and stars, every one of which He sustains and guides with His all-powerful arm. Now if a man, instead of worshipping this Creator God, looks up to the Sun, which He has suspended in our sky as a lamp to lighten the earth, and deluding himself into the belief that that Sun is really God, recites Mantras and addresses prayer to it, he is clearly not a sane person, but a madman utterly bereft of his reason. The Sun is an inanimate substance. It has neither intelligence nor consciousness. Our duty is to worship only God, who is possessed of all wisdom. Leaving Him and doing homage to the Sun is the way to hell. As the Gayatri inculcates the worship of the Sun, it is a lying Mantra, which teaches only the way to perdition. To claim that it will remove sin, and give us heaven is the emptiest of pretensions. The Brahmins, who recite this Mantra every day, are infatuated. By leaving God and adoring a mere luminary, they only add sin to sin and rush madly down the road to hell.

Attend while we give you one more proof, that this Gayatri is a stupendous falsehood.

The Mānava D'harmma Sāstra tells us, that if a Brahmin recites the Gayatri Mantra daily for three years, he will change his form, and becoming endowed with an ethereal air-like body, will be able to roam at will through earth and heaven.* Now, both in town and country, there are hundreds of Brahmins, who, not during three years only but during forty years, have, without once missing, daily repeated this Gayatri Mantra. Of these Brahmins we see many every day laboriously begging from street to street. But who up to this time ever saw a single one among them clothed with an ethereal form or riding fairy-like through the air? Surely we have proof enough, that this Mantra is a bare-faced lie.

THIRD.

Thousands confide in the Panchākshara Mantra, or five-lettered incantation. It is so called because it is made up of the five letters following, namely; Na-ma-Si-vā-ya. Its meaning is, "Salutation to Siva." Devotees of Siva, who wear the Vib'huti or sacred ashes on their foreheads recite this Mantra in worshipping him.

* See Appendix ; page 116.

BRAHMOTTARA KANDAM : PANCHAKSHARA MAHIMAI.

The glory of the five-lettered incantation.

Literal Translation.

" Divine knowledge will come to all, who say Na-ma in the presence of Siva, the Immaculate. Moreover, the eight excellent super-human powers, and heaven (or liberation) will be immediately gained by those who, going to a temple dear to Siva, receive instruction from good priests."

General Meaning.

This verse tells us, that divine knowledge and heaven itself are gained by reciting the Panchākshara Mantra, or " Salutation to Siva."

Is it well blindly to believe all this without consideration? Would it not be wise to inquire first whether it is at all right to offer any salutations whatever to this Siva? Surely you cannot have forgotten how, when you were boys in school studying the Divākaram, you read of this Siva under the name of " Péyōdādi."* You know that he got this name, because placing a snake among his locks, and tying garlands of skulls around his neck, and hanging bones with pigs' teeth upon his breast, and smearing himself all over with ashes, he went and danced with devils and goblins in the place where dead bodies are burned. How, we ask you, can the worship of this dancer with devils produce divine knowledge? How can heaven be the fruit of muttering an incantation associated with the name of such a person? One thing is certain, namely, that falling into hell is the only gain which can possibly accrue to those who trust in Siva, and recite Mantras in his name.

B'HAGAVATA : DASAMA SKANDA.
VIRUKASURANAI KONRA AD'HYAYA.

Literal Translation.

" O thou who art like the thousand-headed Atiséshan ! Can the words of Siva the madman be true, who, decorat-

* " Péyōdādi" means a dancer with devils.

ing his head with a garland of full-blown Erukka flowers,
danced with devils, the place of cremation overspread with
glowing coals serving him for an elegant theatre ? "

General Meaning.

Vishnu addressing Virukāsuran said ; O king ! Are
the statements of the madman Siva, who, decking his
hair with flowers, danced with devils in the place of
cremation, to be believed ? No, they are lies.

FOURTH.

Many people believe in the Ashtākshara Mantra, or
eight-lettered incantation. It is so called, because it is
made up of the eight letters following, namely ; Om-
Na-mō-Nā-rā-ya-nā-ya. Its meaning is " Salutation to
Nārāyana," that is to Vishnu. Devotees of Vishnu,
who wear the Nāmam, or tridental mark on their foreheads, recite this Mantra in worshipping him.

RAMAYANA : YUKTA KANDAM :
HIRAN'YAN VATHAI PADALAM.

Literal Translation.

" That which bestows everything desired ; that which,
when all else ceases, confers blissful heaven ; that which
introduces to the welfare produced by the Homa sacrifice
shooting upward its red flames, is the name of the incomparable god. Hear it. Namō Nārāyanāya."

General Meaning.

This verse tells us, that the Mantra under consideration not only confers everything one wishes for in this
world, but furthermore bestows heaven with all its
untold joys. Vaishnavas believe this empty nonsense,
without the smallest inquiry as to its truth or falsehood. Is it well so to do ? This Mantra is addressed
to Vishnu. But are you not well aware, that this
Vishnu is no other than he, who ravished the cow-
herdesses, and who slew his uncle Kansa, and who stole
milk, butter and curds ? It amazes us, that your lips
consent to call such a one god. This Vishnu is no god.
Reciting Mantras addressed to him is like " tiring the
arm with pounding chalf,"

FIFTH.

Vaishnavas also repeat the word " Rama" as a
Mantra, and declare, without either rhyme or reason,
that it removes all sin, guilt, and evil, and that it com-
fers all merit, glory and good. But what ground is
there for believing all this. The Mantra is addressed
to Rama. Have you not heard that Rama's history?
Failing to protect his wife Sita, he was robbed of her by
the cruel giant Ravana. Unable to discover the place
to which the ravisher had carried her, Rama distract-
ed with grief rushed wildly up and down the forest
bewildered and sobbing, as he fruitlessly searched for
the lost prize. Learning some time afterwards from
the monkey Hanumān, that Sita was imprisoned in
Ceylon, he made various efforts to rescue her, but found
himself unequal to the task. He succeeded at last, only
by securing the aid of Sugreeva and a host of other
monkeys. Such is the tale, as you have often heard
it read on your pials from the pages of the Ramayana.
Answer us candidly now. Is he a god, who derives his
knowledge and his power from monkeys? Is not your
confidence, that this Rama, who had neither wisdom
nor ability enough to save his own wife, can save you,
a worthless confidence? And is it not labor lost to
recite Mantras in his name? Surely your trust in
him will prove as vain as that of " the parrot which
awaited the ripening of the cotton-pods."

Oh People! which of all these various Mantras are
we to accept as the true one ?

"The Gayatri of course" replies the Brahmin,
"Nothing like the Gayatri."

" Sheer nonsense," cries the Saivaite, " the Panchākshara" is immeasurably its superior.

" Mistaken both of you" exclaims the Vaishnava,
" the Ashtakshara Mantra is infinitely more efficacious
than either."

"Away with you all," howls some one else, "the syllable 'Om' is all-sufficient. It is the chief of Mantras. There is nothing that can for a moment be compared with it." Arraigned at the bar of reason, they must all be condemned as equally false and equally worthless.

So some even among yourselves have declared. For example :

Literal Translation.

"Oh my soul! What profits it, that thou wast born in sacred ashes? What that thou hast bathed in holy streams? Thou hast not thereby found the way of changing (thy nature,) or of being born (with a better nature.) Of what use are the seventy million Mantras written in the great Vedas? Still immersed in the river (of the world) thou flounderest about, not knowing how to reach the shore (of heaven.")

General Meaning.

What profits it, oh my soul, that thou hast diligently rubbed ashes and bathed in sacred streams? The means of attaining to a better nature are still unknown to thee. Of what use are the myriads of Vedic Mantras? Ignorant of the landing place, thou art still floundering helplessly in the river of sin.

Oh People! Trust not in these Mantras. They will do you no good, but evil and only evil. If a sick man takes the wrong medicine, his disease instead of being cured is greatly aggravated thereby. Just so your sin, instead of being removed, will be vastly increased by these Mantras. Understand this matter well. Our sins can never be removed either by reciting Mantras, or by any other actions whatsoever, which we may perform.

Some will tell you, that true sorrow for sin effects its removal. But this is also a false doctrine. However many tears we shed, our guilt will not thereby be washed away. A thunder-cloud, having sent forth its bolt of fire, cannot quench it with the rain which it afterwards

J

pours out. So, when once we have committed a sin, we can never wash it away with tears, though they stream in torrents from our weeping eyes.

Beloved! Unless God Himself pardons and removes our sins, they will never be taken away. But there is one great obstacle even to His pardoning and removing them. That obstacle is His infinite justice. A simple illustration will make this plain to you.

Suppose the case of a great king ruling over a vast empire. On a certain occasion, the son of that king is convicted of robbery. Now, however ardently the king may wish to forgive the crime, because the criminal is his own son, would it be right for him so to do? You reply at once, that it would not. And why not? What obstacle is there to his forgiving his son? It is his regal justice, is it not, which stands as an immoveable obstacle in the way? If that king, shewing partiality, should not punish the offender, but pardon him because he is his child, all his subjects would reproach him as destitute of justice. Thus his justice would be ruined; his name would be ruined; and his law would be ruined. And with the ruin of these three, his kingdom would also be ruined.

Oh People! We have broken the laws of God. We have sinned and are guilty. God cannot without doing violence to His justice pardon our sins, unless full satisfaction for them is first made. But He will never do violence to His own justice. Hence we see that God's justice is the great obstacle to His forgiving our sins. And now how is this difficulty to be overcome? Are we able, think you, to satisfy the Divine justice and thus remove the obstacle? Alas! how vain the question. As well ask whether we could with a small needle dig down, remove, and annihilate a vast mountain? As well inquire whether a tiny insect, finding the Himalayas obstructing its path, could lift them on its back, and bearing them aloft through the air cast them into the depths of the sea? Supposing even such things to be possible, it would still be impossible for us to satisfy the justice of an offended God.

By His justice God is bound to condemn us to hell, and punish us there for ever. How then can He at all save us? Is there any way by which God can, without swerving from justice, rescue us from our doom? If there is such a way, His wisdom and His grace will be conspicuous in its discovery.

CURAL; 58TH CHAPTER : 8TH STANZA.

Literal Translation.

" The world rightly belongs to those kings, who are able to shew mercy without injury to their justice."

What Tiruvalluvar here says is true. He tells us that a king, who can exercise mercy without damage to the justice he is bound to execute, is worthy to govern the world. God is the King of kings. By His very nature He is bound always and perfectly to fulfil the demands of His justice. But is there no way by which He can forgive sin without doing violence to that justice? This is the very thing we need to know. There is such a way. Wishing to save us from hell, God has Himself devised and appointed that way. It was for this very purpose, that He sent His Son Jesus Christ into the world. Listen then while we give you a brief account of the advent and the actions of Jesus Christ. It is by Him, that God's justice has been satisfied. It is by Him, that all obstacles to pardon have been removed. It is by Him alone that salvation and heavenly bliss have been procured for us.

This Jesus Christ is the true and eternal God. Many centuries ago, He descended to Earth and became incarnate as a man. He lived in this world thirty-three years. Declaring Himself to be the Saviour of mankind, He taught the doctrines of true knowledge, gathered a company of disciples, and went about doing good. Leading a life of spotless purity, He set it up as a model to be imitated and followed by all. Finally, He voluntarily took upon Himself and endured a fearful punish-

ment. Would you know what it was? Fixed to the
cross with nails driven through His hands and His feet,
He died, having first suffered intolerable agonies. On
the third day bursting the bonds of death He rose
alive from the grave, and trod the earth for forty days.
Then after graciously communicating to His disciples
the words of life, He left this earth, and mounting
through the air returned to the world of heaven.

If you ask why Jesus Christ suffered thus; the
answer is, that He bore upon earth the penalties, which
we, as sinners, deserve to endure in hell. He submitted
to this punishment in order that He might appease the
offended justice of God. By so doing, He made satisfaction to the divine justice, and removed the obstacle,
which stood in the way of God's pardoning guilty men.
He opened the way of salvation to sinners. Because
He thus endured the punishment due to our transgressions, God can bestow pardon, and bestow it without
injury to His justice. And in consequence of this satisfaction made by Jesus Christ, God now speaks gracious
words to the Sons of men. Hear the merciful revela-
tion.

"All who renounce the ways of wickedness and believe
in Jesus Christ shall, for His sake, have their sins pardoned
and their guilt removed. Heaven also with its eternal
unchanging joys shall be conferred upon them."

Precious, life-giving words are these. All who listen
to and accept them will attain to heaven. All others
will fall into hell.

To make this matter clearer, we will tell you a true
story by way of illustration.

Many years ago, there lived in the province of Locria
a good king, who governed his subjects with a just and
even hand. At one period of his reign the crime of
adultery greatly increased in his kingdom. The monarch fearing that both the land and its inhabitants
would be ruined by this vice, and determining if possi-

ble to put a stop to it, made and promulgated the following law, namely; that whoever in future committed adultery should have both his eyes plucked out. For a time, his subjects fearing the threatened penalty strictly observed the law. But afterwards one of them dared to brake it, and having been detected in his sin was dragged into the royal presence. The moment the king looked upon the culprit, he saw that he was no other than his own son, the only heir to his throne and kingdom. Thereupon the king's mind was filled with great fear and consternation. "Alas! Alas!" he thought within himself, "Is this not the child whom I begat, and whom I have so tenderly cherished, my loved son, the apple of my eye, the heir to my name and my kingdom? What alas! shall I do? How can I pluck out the eyes of my own child?" Thus greatly troubled, his heart melted with inexpressible sorrow.

Soon however, he began to reason with himself thus: "If I pardon this culprit and spare his eyes because he is my child, the whole world will reproach me as an unjust prince, and pronounce my government partial and unfair. All my subjects will be emboldened to violate the laws. Order will give place to confusion, and my kingdom will speedily be overthrown. I cannot swerve from justice. The law must have its course. I must execute the penalty, though the sufferer is my beloved child."

Thus was the king's heart torn with contending emotions. On the one side, mercy pleaded hard that his child should be pardoned; on the other, justice sternly demanded the punishment of the offender. At last the king began to consider whether there might not be some middle course, whereby he might satisfy the requirements both of his mercy and his justice, without doing violence to either. "Oh!" thought he, "if I could only vindicate my justice, and yet pardon my child, how joyful I should be."

Suddenly a happy expedient darted into his mind. His face beaming with smiles, he mounted the throne, and ordered the case to be tried. Witnesses were examined and the prisoner being found guilty of adultery, sentence was at the king's command pronounced. The culprit was according to the law condemmed to have his two eyes plucked out. Thereupon the king spoke as follows: " Listen, Oh Counsellors, Princes, and People ! The law must be executed, and justice must be fulfilled Two eyes must be plucked out. But hear what I have to say. This is my son. Bound together by the bonds of blood and of affection, he and I are as one. Therefore an eye of his, and an eye of mine shall pay the penalty of the law." So saying, the king, having caused an eye of his son to be plucked out, plucked out one of his own and laid them side by side. Then resuming his address he said, " The penalty has been executed. See, here are the two eyes plucked out. I have vindicated the majesty of the law. Justice and Mercy triumph together inviolate. I have saved my child, but without injury to the statute. Therefore let none henceforward dare to violate it, for you now see that my justice is unbending, while my mercy is great." Then every mouth was filled with plaudits. Perceiving how signally the king had shewed mercy without prejudice to justice, his subjects lauded his wisdom, extolled his mercy, feared his equity, and yielded themselves a thousand times more submissively to his government than before.

And now, why did this king pluck out one of his own eyes ? Why did he, the guiltless, thus suffer punishment for his guilty son ? Was it not that he might thereby honor his law, vindicate his justice, and at the same time save his child ? This is precisely what Jesus Christ has done for us. To magnify the Divine law, to preserve inviolate the Divine justice, and yet at the same time to rescue sinful men, he came and suffered and died in their stead. Oh People ! May you, believing on Him as your Saviour, through Him reach the blissful shores of heaven !

APPENDIX to NO. VII.

Examples and Illustrations.

(1.) Vedic ceremonies will all perish; but the Mantra "Om" never. It is itself God.

Menu 2; 84.

Literal Translation.

"The Homa with all other Vedic sacrifices and ceremonies must perish. Let it be known that the Pranava is indestructible. (If it be asked why, it) is Brahm, the Supreme Lord of all."

General Meaning.

Vedic ceremonies must all perish. But the Pranava can never perish, because it is itself God.

(2.) The four Vedas sprung from the Mantra Om. He, who knows it, knows all things. Women and Sudras may not repeat it.

Anonymous Stanza.

Literal Translation.

" As the (great) Banian tree springs from a (small) seed, so the Vedas and the Sastras spring from the word Om. Whoever pronounces the word Om pronounces all the Vedas and all the Sastras. Whoever knows the meaning of the word Om knows certainly all the Vedas and all the Sastras. Excepting the word Om, the Panchākashara may be taught to women and law abiding Sudras."

General Meaning.

The Vedas with all the other Sastras sprung from the Mantra Om. Those who have mastered its meaning have mastered the meaning of all the Sastras. It must never be taught to women or Sudras.

This verse affirms that the four Vedas derived their being from the Mantra Om. But in direct contradiction to this, the Mānava Dharmma Sastra (Chapter 2nd; Stanza 79th) declares, that Brahma milked the Mantra Om out of three Vedas.

(3.) By repeating the Gayatri a thousand times, all sin will be removed within a month.

MENU 2 : 79.

Literal Translation.

" If a Brahmin, apart from the multitude, recites these three (viz. Om, Vyāhruti, and Gayatri) a thousand times, he will within a month be released from great sin, as a serpent from his slough."

General Meaning.

If a Brahmin repeats the Om, Vyāhruti and Gayatri Mantras a thousand times, the great sins committed by him will be removed within a month.

(4.) Whatever else one may or may not do; if he only repeats the Gayatri, he will gain heaven.

MENU 2 : 87.

Literal Translation.

" It is by reciting the Gayatri, that a Brahmin gets heaven. Of this there is no doubt. It matters not whether he does or does not do anything else. If he be friendly to all, he is (justly) called a Brahmin."

General Meaning.

If a Brahmin only recites the Gayatri, it matters not whether he does or does not do other things : he is sure to reach heaven.

(5.) If a Brahmin repeats the Gayatri Mantra daily for three years, he will change his form, and acquiring an ethereal air-like body will be able to roam everywhere at will.

MENU 2 : 82.

Literal Translation.

" Whoever without remissness recites this (Gayatri) daily for three years, will become like the air, and possessed of an ethereal body will attain to the supreme Brahm."

General Meaning.

The Brahmin, who repeats the Gayatri Mantra every day for three years, will become like the air, and will with an ethereal body reach God.

SCRIPTURE TEXTS.

(1.) God abhors all incantations.
Deut. 18. 10, 11, 12. Isaiah 8. 19, 20. Mat. 6. 7.
(2.) The Sun Moon and Stars are not to be worshipped.

Deut. 4. 19. Job 31. 26 to 28.
Deut. 17. 2 to 5. Ezek. 8. 15, 16.

(3.) God delights in the prayers of the faithful.
Psalm 145. 18, 19. Mat. 7. 7 to 11. 1 Peter 3. 12.
(4.) How prayer is to be made.

Mat. 6. 6 to 13. Mark 11. 25.
Jer. 29. 13. Mat. 21. 22.

ADDRESS No. VIII.

TRANSMIGRATION.

THE Ṣastras of this country teach that there are many successive births, and its people generally accept this teaching as true. They believe that the human soul, immediately upon leaving one body, enters into some other form, and so in endless transmigration continues for myriads of years to pass through many successive births.

NALLA PILLAI B'HARATA: ARAN'YA PARUVAM:
. KOUSIKA SARUKKAM.

Literal Translation.

" Souls, if their good actions exceed, will obtain celestial bodies. If their actions are good and bad mixed together, they will enter into complex human bodies. If their evil actions exceed, they will pass into the forms of trees, beasts, and other inferior living beings, moveable and immoveable. So say the wise."

General Meaning.

In this verse we are told, that the soul of one, who has done "good actions" abundantly, will be born as a god; that the soul of one, who has performed "good actions" and "evil actions" in about equal proportions, will be born as a man; and that the soul of one, whose "evil actions" exceed, will be born as a tree, or as a beast.

Again, in the twelfth Ad'hyaya of the MānavaDharmma Ṣastra, we find some exceedingly marvellous particulars. Entering largely into details, it tells us that man will be born as a dog, a pig, an ass, a camel, a bullock, a sheep, a deer, a worm, an insect, a fly, a spider, a snake, a crocodile, a grass, a shrub, a creeper, an eagle, a lion, a tiger, a cat, a mongoose, a frog, a lizard, a peacock, a monkey, a fish, a tortoise, a jackal, a gnat, and in various other forms too numerous to mention.*

Oh People! Do you really believe, that the soul of man, losing its human nature and properties, is going to be born in these multitudinous forms? What strange hallucination is this? From one point of view, it looks like a story told merely to frighten little children; and from another point of view, like a fable calculated to make those same little ones laugh and frisk about with glee. Which of the two is the more correct does not clearly appear. While listening to it, we can hardly repress our inclination to laugh. But after a moment's thought, it seems much more appropriate to mourn and weep over the sad fact, that intelligent human beings allow themselves to be deceived and ruined by such ridiculous trash.

You affirm, that men pass through many and various births or transmigrations. But what proof do you give of this? You cannot of course expect us to believe such a story on your mere say-so. Some of you will doubtless answer the question by saying:

"*Our Sastras are authority for the truth of this doctrine.*"

But unfortunately your Sastras are replete with mis-statements and falsehoods. Take one example only out of many.

Nalla Pillai B'harata: Ati Paruvam: Garuda Sarukkam.

Literal Translation.

"Rāhu and Kétu having, by virtue of the power derived from eating Ambrosia, performed (otherwise) impossible penances, obtained from Siva the boon of alternately swallowing and vomiting the Sun and the Moon. In consequence of this arrangement, the gods (undisturbedly) ate the cool Ambrosia to their hearts' content."

The Maha B'harata also, which you extol as a fifth Veda, tells us, that Siva conferred upon the two serpents

* See Appendix, page 132.

Ráhu and Kétu the gift of alternately swallowing and ejecting the Sun and the Moon ; and that solar and lunar eclipses are the result of this engorging and disgorging process. The very idea of a snake crawling up the sky, seizing the Sun in its jaws, swallowing and then vomiting forth that luminary has in it something irresistibly ludicrous. Many of your children even, who attend school, know perfectly well, that this story is an unmitigated falsehood. One of your proverbs says that " the more you break and examine a fig, the more worms you find." So the more closely you scrutinize your Sastras, the more lies you will discover in them. And is it these Sastras, overburdened as they are with such stupendous falsehoods, that you bring to us as reliable authorities ? Know that they can never answer your purpose. Sastras, which stand convicted of telling one lie about a snake's swallowing the Sun, may reasonably be suspected of telling another, when they affirm the existence of many births. Hence their authority is worthless, and wise men will never admit them in evidence.

Your Sastras having thus been proved to be incompetent authority, we ask for other and better proof than they can afford of the reality of Transmigration. To this some will perhaps reply, that,

" *Successive births are the appointed rewards of virtue and of vice.*"

To many it seems a natural and excellent rule, that virtue and vice should meet their appropriate recompense in succeeding births. Hence they use this as an argument to prove the doctrine of Transmigration. We find this ground taken in the Mahá B'harata, as follows.

NALLA PILLAI B'HARATA : ASVAMED'HA PARUVAM :
KRISHNARJUNA SAMAVADA SARUKKAM.

Literal Translation.

" All actions done in this world belong to (one of) two classes, namely sin and virtue. These are the seeds, which produce (respectively) sorrow and joy. Moreover it is in consequence of those actions, that souls take bodies. So say the wise."

General Meaning.

Successive births have been ordained, in order that vice may be punished, and virtue meet with its proper reward. Such is the substance of this verse.*

Furthermore, detailed rules are laid down as to the particular penalties which follow particular crimes. For example.

NALLA PILLAI B'HARATA : ANUSASANIKA PARUVAM : ASARAM URAITTA SARUKKAM.

Literal Translation.

" If a man steals oil, ghee, or anything else from a temple, he will die, and being born as a bandycoote or a pig will suffer greatly. After many days passed in one of these forms, he will enter successively and continuously into the bodies of dogs and other animals. Know this, O thou who art learned."

General Meaning.

This verse tells us, that a man, who steals oil or ghee belonging to a temple, will after death be born as a bandycoote or a pig, and, after having endured much suffering for a long period in one of these forms, will again be born as a dog.

Let us look into this a little. Does the soul, when it is born as a bandycoote, know that it was once in a human body, that it then stole ghee, and that, as a punishment for the theft, it is now born as a bandycoote? Assuredly the bandycoote knows nothing whatever about all this. It is entirely ignorant both that it formerly stole in human form, and that it is now roaming about as a bandycoote in punishment for the theft. How then can this be called a punishment at all? Even allowing it to be a species of punishment, what propriety is there in the method of it? If it becomes necessary to punish any one, it is no more than right, that he should be made acquainted with his fault before the penalty is

---

* See Appendix, page 133.

K

inflicted. Punishing, without first showing the offender his crime, is wrong. What justice then, or what profit is there in punishing a soul by catching and shutting it up in a bandycoote's body, where it cannot by any possibility know either that it has ever committed a fault, or that it is now suffering the penalty due to that fault? There is no justice in it. Neither is it, strictly speaking, a punishment at all; for the soul is, in that form, utterly incapable of recognizing it as such. Is it this then of which you boast as a "natural and excellent rule" of punishment? God has made no such unjust and profitless rule. He has appointed no such penalties as these for the human soul. The great Lord, who punishes human souls, always punishes them in ways fitted not only to make them recognize their faults, but also to see the righteous connection between those faults, and the penalties He inflicts. Hence your affirmation, that Transmigration is a divinely appointed punishment of sin, is only vain talk. It is a mere fable concocted by foolish men.

Equally vain is it to assert, that a good birth is the reward of good deeds. For in this case also, the soul, which is said to have entered such a birth, is not in the least aware either that it formerly performed good deeds, or that its present happy condition is the fruit of those good deeds. It has not even the faintest recollection of a previous state of being. And, as a matter of course, it cannot know, that in consequence of such and such good deeds previously performed, it is now enjoying such and such remunerations. Hence there is no such thing as reward in the case. The very idea of a reward necessarily involves on the part of him who receives it a double knowledge, namely; first, that he has performed a certain action; and secondly, that what he receives is the fruit of that action. But all such knowledge is clearly wanting here. Hence it is absurd and false to speak of Transmigration as the reward of vice and virtue.

Some among you offer still another argument for Transmigration, which is as follows;

The soul being defiled with sin, Transmigration has been appointed as the means of cleansing and purifying it.

In the 56th Sloka of the 12th Ad'hyaya of the Mānava Dharmma Sastra,* it is stated, that a Brahmin who drinks arrack will hereafter be born as a worm, or an insect, or a grasshopper, or a bird feeding on ordure, or a beast of prey.

How the soul of a toddy-drinking Brahmin is to lose its sin-stains and become purified by any of the above-mentioned births does not very readily appear. For example, how in reason is his soul to become clean by his being born as a carrion-crow, and gulping down all the filth he lights upon? Besides, if eating filth is all that is required, why become a crow for that? Why not force himself somehow or other to swallow the filth at once, and thus purify his soul while he is yet in his Brahmin form?

But listen further. The Mānava Dharmma Sastra, in the 62nd Sloka of its 12th Ad'hyaya† speaks as follows. If one steals paddy, he will be born a rat: if he steals bell-metal, he will be born a gander: if he steals water, he will be born a frog: if he steals honey, he will be born a gnat: if he steals milk, he will be born a crow: if he steals juice, he will be born a dog: and if he steals ghee, he will be born a mongoose. In a following Sloka, it is said, that if he steals fruit, he will be born a monkey.

Now consider what sort of teaching this is. We are told that if a man has stolen paddy, he must, in order to cleanse his soul of this fault, be born as a rat, a creature whose chief occupation is, as we all know, to steal paddy. Or if he has stolen fruit, he must, in order to expiate this crime, be born a monkey, the animal which above all others is for ever stealing fruit. In other words, a man must, by way of atoning for one act of

* See Appendix, page 133.

† See Appendix, page 134.

theft, become an eternal thief. This country excepted, there is no place in the wide world, where such a doctrine as this is even heard of. All this being so, does it not sound very much like blasphemy to say, that God has ordained Transmigration as a means of purifying the soul?

Again we ask you, what proof is there of the existence of Transmigration? Not one. Reflect a little. If you yourselves have existed in a previous birth, how comes it, that you have no remembrance, however slight, of it now? Surely there ought to be at least some faint floating reminiscence of having been in such a state. For example, if in a previous birth you were a lion, we should naturally expect to find in you now some small remnant of leonine pride, as you remember, however faintly, that you roamed lord of such and such a forest, and exultingly selected your prey from among beasts helplessly affrighted by your terrible roars. Or if in a previous birth you were a donkey, we should not unreasonably look for some trifling residue of asinine shame, as, you recall, however indistinctly, the fact that in such a town you were cruelly beaten by pitiless washermen, while you laboriously staggered under vast bundles of clothes. Or if in a previous birth you were a dog, we should fairly count upon seeing in you a relic or so of canine servility, as you recollect, however vaguely, that you wagged your tail in such a house of such a village. Or if in a previous birth, you were a Brahmin, we should legitimately reckon upon detecting a trace or two of Brahminical trickery, as you call to mind, however obscurely, that in such a district you lived luxuriously and bore yourself haughtily, while you were all the time filling your belly by deceiving and cheating the poor. But we discover nothing of the kind. Who can say that he was formerly in such and such a birth, and lived in such and such a way? You cannot find one who will venture to do it. There is not the smallest trace of such a remembrance in anybody's mind.

It will not answer to say here, that you have forgotten those things, just as you have forgotten things which occurred in your infancy. It is quite true that you cannot remember matters which took place during your infancy in this present birth ; and, by parity of reasoning, it could not be accounted wonderful, that you should fail to recall the occurrences of infancy in a former birth. But if you really existed in a former birth, you surely were not infants throughout its entire duration. Did you not then grow into youth ? Did you not attain to manhood ? Did you not marry ? Did you not work hard for a living ? Did you not laboriously support your children ? Did you not feel hunger and thirst, disease and pain ? Did you not experience joys and sorrows innumerable ? Can it be possible that you have entirely forgotten all this ? Oh People ! Why do you believe such glaring falsehoods as these ? Surely the thoughts and words and deeds of a previous existence could not all have thus passed into one common and total oblivion. Get understanding and learn the truth. Know clearly, that neither previous births nor subsequent births have any existence whatsoever.

Compare, in this connection, the operations of nature. Look at the plantain tree growing in your gardens, for even that may afford you useful instruction. It grows, shoots out its leaves, yields its rich cluster of fruit, and then fading dies. Does any one imagine, that after thus dying the same plantain tree will again spring up and live upon the earth ? No. What then ? Before it dies, it sends forth young suckers from its roots. When the parent-tree is dead, its offspring, standing in the place it occupied, grow and bear fruit in their turn. But the parent-tree can never live again. Just so a man begets children and dies. Those children occupy the place he once occupied, and perpetuate his family. But as for him once dead, he can never again be born and live upon the earth.

Attend now to some arguments we are about to set before you. Our object shall be to prove, that the doctrine of Transmigration is a most pernicious doctrine.

FIRST.

If the doctrine of Transmigration be true, the way to heaven is effectually closed against all mankind.

The 58th Sloka, of the 12th Chapter of the Mānava Dharmma Sastra* says, that he, who violates the bed of his Guru, will be born a hundred times in the forms of grasses, of shrubs, of creeping plants, of vultures, and of wild beasts.

Now if this is to be believed, all grasses, shrubs, creeping plants, and trees upon the face of the earth are nothing else than human souls. And if so, what right have we to eat greens, vegetables, and pot-herbs? Are not all who eat them murderers? Yet you eat them continually. Every day of your lives, you seize and pluck up and kill those poor souls, you plunge them into water, build a fire under them, and boil them, you bite them with your teeth, and taste them with your palates, you swallow them down your gullets, and digest them in your stomachs. What a fearfully atrocious sin! Moreover, this is not the sin of a single day; but it is a series of murders which you are committing day after day, and many times in each day of your lives. As many leaves, as many stalks, as many greens, as many fruits ripe and unripe as you have ever plucked and eaten, so many souls you have murdered and devoured.

But you will say, that greens and vegetables and fruit are essential food. We must eat them or die. If men should cease to eat them, the whole world would shortly be depopulated. True. And does not this very show you, that the doctrine of Transmigration is a lie? For who is it, that has made vegetables and fruit necessary to human life? And who is it, that has given them

---

* See Appendix : page 194.

to us as food? Is it not God Himself? If they are truly re-born human souls, would He, think you, give them to us as food? Or would He, think you, have so created us, that we must either eat them or die? Moreover if those vegetables are souls, the whole human race are forced, by the very necessities of their nature, to murder and devour them every day of their lives. Not a single man can by any possibility cease from committing the sin, and of course not a single man can ever get to heaven. Would God ordain so vast an iniquity? Never. Hence we are sure that trees and vegetables are not the souls of departed men. Eat them we may and lawfully, for God has given them to us to eat. Hence the doctrine of Transmigration is a false doctrine.

SECOND.

THE DOCTRINE OF TRANSMIGRATION ENCOURAGES MEN TO SIN.

The adherents of this doctrine teach, that all the desires and all the conduct of a man in his present birth are the necessary and inevitable results of his actions in a former birth. Now the belief of such teaching cannot fail to produce large harvests of sin. It makes men reason as follows:—"Although the desire I now feel is a wicked desire, yet I may indulge it, for is it not the fated and unavoidable fruit of my deeds performed in a previous birth?"—And so this belief causes them to plunge recklessly into sin. Nothing can be more certain, than that this doctrine, which ruins men by thus forcibly dragging them into wicked practices, is not from God; but is a false doctrine devised and promulgated by evil men.

THIRD.

THIS DOCTRINE, BESIDES ENCOURAGING MEN TO SIN, SHUTS THEM UP, AS IT WERE, TO ITS COMMISSION.

The Bible reveals, that, on the death of the body, the soul immediately enters upon its eternal state either of happiness in heaven, or of misery in hell. If this

doctrine is taught to men, there is reasonable ground
of hope, that they, becoming alarmed at the fatal consequences of sin, will relinquish it, and seek the way to
heaven.   But if, on the contrary, men are taught to believe, that they must inevitably pass through myriads
of successive births; the natural consequence is, that
they become unconcerned about their future happiness.
" Let that come, which must come.   What can we do ?
Do what we may, there is no possibility of escaping our
predestined births.   What then is the use of thinking
about the matter ?   Whether we do right or do wrong,
it cannot alter our fate."   Thus reasoning with themselves, they will never leave off sinning.   They will
never inquire the way to heaven, nor seek forgiveness
of God ; but, on the contrary, continue walking unconcerned in the ways of sin.   A doctrine, which thus shuts
men up as it were to the commission of sin, cannot be
from God.   It is plainly a false doctrine, which bears
every appearance of having emanated from wicked men
and devils joined together in rebellion against God.

Hear what one of your sages says about those, who
teach this false and pernicious doctrine.

Translation.

" The Gurus of this world, discoursing about the two-fold
actions, declare on the authority of the Vedas, that when
the soul at death leaves the body, which it is now wearing
as the result of its deeds in a former birth, it will enter upon
a new birth and appear again clothed in another body.
What ! can that, which has already once entered the womb,
been born upon earth, and after the lapse of a hundred years
passed away from it, be born again as an infant ? Consider,
my masters ! the immense wealth, which these Gurus plunder from their ignorant disciples by terrifying them with
this doctrine of future births."

A careful consideration of these various arguments
cannot fail to convince you, that there is no such thing
as a Transmigration of souls.

But some of you will perhaps here ask the question,
' Are there then no fruits whatever following upon good

and evil actions?" A useful inquiry, and one which we are most desirous of answering. Such fruits there undoubtedly are. Eternal heaven is the fruit of good actions. Eternal hell is the fruit of evil actions. When a man dies, it is not his soul, but his body only that perishes. The soul can never die. Immediately on the death of the body, the soul passes either into heaven or into hell. Whichever place it enters, there it must for ever stay. If it reaches heaven, there it will always remain, associated with eternal joy, and experiencing unceasing transports of bliss. In that world there is no pain, no sorrow, no want. If it falls into hell, there it will always continue, associated with eternal sorrow, and enduring everlasting torments, as it rolls with devils and fiends in a sea of unquenchable fire. In that world, there is no comfort, no joy. Beloved! Is it not both wise and good, that we should, one and all, strive earnestly to escape from hell, and attain to the eternal comforts and felicities of heaven?

How then can we escape hell, and how reach heaven? This is what we need, above all else, to know. Some will tell us, that the performance of meritorious actions will accomplish the end we have in view. But listen attentively, while we discuss this point a little at large. A meritorious person, properly so called, is one, who never having once broken the laws of God in thought word or deed, has from the moment of his birth continued perfectly holy both in his dispositions and in his conduct. Such a one would certainly be worthy of heaven, and would obtain unobstructed entrance there. But where shall we look for such a man? In what land, or among what people can such a one be discovered? Alas! there is not in the wide world a single meritorious person. We have all done evil actions. Being sinners, our dispositions are all sinful dispositions. Our soul is a sinful soul. Actions good and entitling us to heaven can by no possibility spring from a sinful soul. We are utterly without power to perform such actions.

Thus all mankind are lying ruined in their sins.
Death comes swiftly on. Hell is in their front with
mouth opened to swallow them up. The sin they have
committed stands ready to hurl them down into its
awful depths. To remove that sin, they have no power.
To escape that hell, they can find no way among themselves. There is a heaven, a world of bliss; but they
cannot reach it, for they are destitute not only of the
merit which could bring them there, but also of all
power to procure such merit for themselves. Alas! how
utterly ruined is their condition.

Oh People! Listen now to good tidings sent to you
by a gracious God. There is one, who can remove and
abolish our sins. There is one, who came to Earth and
accumulated merit sufficient for us all. If we do but
obtain that merit, it will of itself shut for us the door
of hell. It will close the mouth of the horrible pit. It
will rescue us from the way of destruction. It will
destroy the sins, which stand ready to push us into
perdition. It will open for us the gates of Paradise.
It will lead us into the way of life. It will bring
us into eternal felicity. Renouncing then all manner
of sin, let us at once seek to obtain that merit for ourselves.

But who is this of whom we speak? What His
name? Where His dwelling place? In what way has
He procured merit for us? How may we know Him?
How reach Him? Attend while we answer these great
questions.

His name is Jesus Christ. He is the one true Lord
and Guru. He is God's only begotten Son. He is the
Ruler of the three worlds. How shall we attempt to
describe the dwelling place of Him, whom the heaven
of heavens cannot contain? He is the all-pervading
Deity, yet he dwells graciously in the hearts of those
who put their trust in Him. God the Father seeing
the entire human race ruined by sin, pitied them and
sent this Jesus Christ His only Son into the world as a
Saviour. Thus sent, He came many years ago to earth

and assuming our nature became incarnate as a man. This is the true Avatar. Jesus Christ appeared God and man in one person upon earth. He dwelt in our world thirty-three years. He performed deeds of mercy wherever He went. He taught true wisdom, and revealed the substance of the true Veda. He blessed all, who sought His favor. The blind, the deaf, and the dumb came and worshipped Him. Worshipping they saw, they heard, they spoke and went away rejoicing. Cripples, paralytics, and lepers cried to Him and were restored. Men besought Him to raise even their dead to life: He commanded, and their dead lived again. By such miracles as these, He openly proved Himself to be God, and many believing adored Him as God. Finally after enduring great suffering, He gave His life for the life of men.

If now you ask how it was possible for one so holy and so meritorious to suffer and to die; we reply, that it was because He took our sins upon Himself, as if they had been His own sins. He, who was without sin, carried the burden of our sin. That we might escape the punishment of hell, He bore for us a terrible punishment upon earth. He voluntarily sustained the penalty due to us. That penalty He experienced both in His soul, and in His body. The divine wrath, which should have cast us into hell, swept like a raging flood over His soul, producing in Him mental anguish so intense, that His sweat was as it were great drops of blood falling down to the ground. He suffered punishment also in His body, which was fixed to the cross with nails driven through His sacred hands and feet. He died undergoing excruciating agonies. Then the Sun became darkened, lacking courage to look upon the sight. The sorrowing Earth trembled and quaked. Rocks sympathizing with His broken heart, rent asunder. Jesus Christ endured all those sufferings on account of His love to us. There was in Him nothing that merited punishment. The penalty He suffered belonged to us. The sin He carried was our sin. He bore those agonies, in order that He might rescue us from hell, and bring us to heaven. Thus He opened the way of expiating our sins. On the third day after death, He rose again with life and majesty from the tomb. During forty following days, he walked and taught upon earth. Then He ascended up through the air to heaven, where He now sits in glory. Thus we have briefly told you how Jesus Christ came to earth, was born as a man, lived a life of spotless purity, bore the sufferings due to us, gave His life as a sacrifice for our sins, rose again from the dead, and returned to the world of heaven. All this constitutes the merit, which He has procured in our behalf. It is merit fitted to save our souls. Would you know this Jesus Christ; seek Him in the Bible. Would you become possessors of His merit; exercise faith in Him as your only Saviour.

Oh People! The Christian Veda is the only true Veda. All others are false. Read that true Veda with your eyes, hear it with your ears, ponder it in your hearts, and walk as it directs you. Then you will know the all-meritorious Guru Jesus Christ. Believe in Him. Leave off all sinful practices. Mourn and weep over the sins you have hitherto committed. Offer your heart as an oblation to Christ. Trust in Him as your God, and your merit-giving Guru, love Him, cling to Him as your only hope, pray to Him at all times, and walk according to His blessed Word. If you do so, He will never suffer you to fall into hell; but will surely bring you to heaven, that you may be there for ever with Himself in bliss.

APPENDIX to No. VIII.

EXAMPLES AND ILLUSTRATIONS.

(1.) For sins connected with the body, man will be born as a vegetable or mineral: for sins connected with the mouth, as a bird or beast: for sins connected with the soul, as a human out-cast.

MENU 12: 9.

Literal Translation.

"For sinful acts springing from the body, a man shall assume a vegetable or mineral form; for sinful acts springing from the mouth, the form of a bird or beast; for sinful acts springing from the mind, the form of a low-caste person."

General Meaning.

For bodily offences, man shall be born a vegetable or a mineral; for verbal offences, a bird or a beast; for mental offences, an out-cast.

(2.) Subsequent births are appointed as the rewards of sinful and meritorious actions.

MENU 12: 74.

Literal Translation.

" By continuing the practice of sinful actions, foolish persons experience sorrows in the various births, (into which they enter) upon earth."

General Meaning.

Foolish souls, by continuing in the practice of sin, suffer, migrating through many births.

(3.) Various mean births resulting from theft.

MENU 12: 67.

Literal Translation.

" If one steals a deer or an elephant, he will be born a wolf; if a horse, a tiger; if fruit or roots, a monkey; if a woman, a bear; if water, a Jātaka bird; if vehicles, a camel; if cattle, a goat."

General Meaning.

Thieves are re-born in the lowest conditions.

(4.) Transmigration ordained for the cleansing of the soul.

MENU 12: 56.

Literal Translation.

" A Brahmin, who drinks arrack, will migrate into the form of a worm or insect, of a fly feeding on ordure, or of some ravening beast."

General Meaning.

If a Brahmin drinks spirituous liquors, he is doomed to be born a worm or insect, a filthy fly or a ravaging beast.

(5.)   Thieves will be born as rats, crows, and the like.

MENU 12 : 62.

Literal Translation.

" If a man steal grain, he will be born a rat ; if bell-metal, a gander : if water, a diving-bird ; if honey, a gnat ; if milk, a crow ; if expressed juice, a dog ; if ghee, a mongoose."

General Meaning.

Stealers of grain, bell-metal, water, honey, milk, expressed juice, and ghee will respectively be born as rats, ganders, divers, gnats, crows, dogs and mongooses.

(6.)   He who sins with his Guru's wife will be born a hundred times as grass, shrubs and so forth.

MENU 12 : 58.

Literal Translation.

" He, who goes in to his Guru's wife, will be born a hundred times in the forms of grasses, shrubs, and twining plants, of carnivorous animals, of beasts with sharp teeth, and of other cruel brutes."

General Meaning.

If a man violates his Guru's wife, he will be born a hundred times as a plant, or as a wild beast.

SCRIPTURE TEXTS.

(1.)   There is no Transmigration.

         Hebrews 9. 27.   Luke 16. 22, 23.
         Job 7. 9, 10.   Luke 23. 43.
         Job 14. 10, 11, 12.   2 Samuel 12. 23.

(2.)   God will recompense every man according to his deeds.

         2 Corinthians 5. 10.   Revelations 20. 11 to 15.
         Romans 2. 5 to 11.   Matthew 25. 31 to 46.
         Galatians 6. 7, 8.   Revelations 21. 8.

ADDRESS No. IX.

~~~~~~~~~

FATE.

In this country, certain men of bewildered intellects and darkened understandings have invented a falsehood, to which they have given the name of Fate. Declaring that all events whatsoever are determined by inexorable Destiny, they, by teaching this pernicious doctrine, bring ruin not only upon themselves, but also upon all others, who are weak enough to be persuaded by their mischievous representations.

They teach, that men are moved and governed by Fate, as a puppet is by its string; and that our thoughts, words and actions are not from ourselves, but are the unavoidable effects of an irresistible Necessity.

Vast numbers of Hindus, accepting this doctrine as true, become utterly unconcerned about their future state. To urge upon such persons the duty of making efforts to escape hell and gain heaven is all in vain. Their invariable reply is, "What can we do? Whatever Fate has decreed must of necessity befal us." Fate, Fate is all their cry. Fate, Fate is the one great excuse, dwelling evermore on the tips of their tongues.

Those, who hold to this wicked doctrine, will never seek the good of their souls. Though one give them advice, they will not listen to it. Though one shew them God's Holy Word, they will not regard it. "If my soul is destined to be saved, it will be saved: if it is destined to be lost, it will be lost. There is no need of any effort on my part. For who can hinder Fate? Who can change its decrees?" Thus reasoning, they decline making any efforts whatever to escape hell, and reach heaven.

Furthermore, this evil doctrine emboldens men to plunge heedlessly into sin. "It matters not," say they, "what we do; for all actions, be they good or evil, are predetermined by irrevocable Fate." And so they dare to commit the worst of crimes. Who can measure the pernicious results of such a doctrine; a doctrine, which, while it robs men of all encouragement to practice virtue, emboldens them to plunge heedlessly and wallow shamelessly in the sinks of vice. If this doctrine is indeed true, of what use soever is the Veda? Of what use the worship of God? Of what use piety and virtue? Why should one trouble himself about such things? A man is not to be blamed though he cast off every restraint, and, giving full swing to his lusts, indulge in all manner of vice; for this also is inexorable Fate. Hence he may drink and riot, he may kill and rob, in short he may commit at will any and every sort of wickedness.

You affirm, that every event is determined by Fate. But what proof can you give of this? Produce your arguments, if you have any.

Perhaps some of you will say "There is 'the writing on the head'; Brahma has inscribed each man's destiny on his skull."

But have you never heard what happened to this same Brahma, who you say fixes the destinies of others? Hear what your Sastra relates about him.

SKANDA PURANA: DAKSHA KANDAM: UTTARA PADALAM.

Literal Translation.

" When Vishnu the Earth-Measurer reached the vast city, Bhairava (i. e. Siva) pinched off with his finger nails the radiant central head of Brahma. Streams of blood gushing forth encircled the world, and the lotus-dwelling Brahma fell fainting.

General Meaning.

This stanza relates that Siva, taking the form of Bhairava, tore off with his nails one of Brahma's heads;

whereupon Brahma, exhausted by the vast torrents of blood gushing from the wound, fell and expired.

How is this? It cannot be possible, that this Brahma, who you say writes every man's fate in visible characters on his head, forgot to write a good fate on his own. He who allots to the inhabitants of all worlds their destinies, would surely manage somehow or other to inscribe a propitious destiny on his own pate; for "None ever take medicine to kill themselves." But in spite of all his writing, he lost, as you see, his head. This loss, it is evident, Brahma did not foresee. But how, we ask, can one, who does not foresee what is going to happen to himself, foresee what is going to happen to others? And if the destiny he inscribed on his own head was reversed, how in reason are the destinies he inscribes on the heads of others to stand?

Hear yet another thing related of this Brahma, whom you call the Arbiter of Fate.

SEVVANTI PURANA : BRAHMA DEVAN ASATTIYAN TIRNTA SARUKKAM.

Literal Translation.

" Siva, who rides the mountain-like bull, becoming enraged cursed Brahma as follows :—Oh thou, who dwellest in the lotus, whose thousand petals close at sight of the Moon! Be thou henceforth unworshipped. Thy creative function also we have abolished.—Thereupon Brahma affrighted fell fainting at the feet of the Cassia-crowned Siva."

General Meaning.

On Brahma's falsely declaring, that he had discovered Siva's head; Siva becoming enraged cursed Brahma to the effect, that thenceforward he should be deprived of creative power and cease to be worshipped as a god.

Here your own Sastra informs you, that Brahma told a lie, and was cursed for telling it. How then, though he write ever so much on your heads, can you place any dependence on that writing?

Again, the assertion that there is "writing on the head" proceeds solely from a want of knowledge. Do you really think, that the lines and marks traceable on the skull are letters? Have you ever examined them closely? They are not letters; but simply lines of junction between bone and bone. The skull is not a single bone; but is made up of several bones articulated with each other. Wherever these bones unite one with another, lines of junction are of course visible. Looking at these lines from a distance, you, without at all ascertaining their real nature, pronounce them at random to be writing. But how foolish this is! Suppose some silly person, on seeing two boards skillfully united by a carpenter, should point to the line of their junction, and pronounce it to be writing; would you not laugh at him? Of course you would. And now tell us if the whole world has not an equal right to laugh, when you gravely assert, that "the writing on the skull" is a proof of the existence of Fate?

Oh People! What is this Fate, which you so groundlessly extol? Is it a god? What you say of it would certainly lead us to think, that you regard it as a sort of divinity. But in the light of reason, it appears at once in its true nature, a monstrous fable. The assertion, that Brahma is the Lord of Fate, has by previous arguments been proved wholly inadmissible. And yet, notwithstanding all that can be said, some will doubtless persist in declaring, that any how there is such a thing as Fate, and that it is of divine appointment. Hence we shall now proceed to prove by various arguments, that this position is, equally with the other, wholly untenable.

FIRST.

To SAY THAT EVERY EVENT IS DETERMINED BY FATE IS EQUIVALENT TO SAYING, THAT GOD HIMSELF IS THE AUTHOR OF SIN.

If God is, in your sense, the supreme arbiter and predeterminer of all actions whatsoever; it follows, that

He is the cause of the wicked actions of men. Again, if He is the cause of the wicked actions of men, it equally follows that men are not sinners, but that God Himself is the Author of sin. But is it right to speak thus of God? Those who speak thus are blasphemers against Him. They are the greatest of sinners, and will fall into the fire of hell. God is not the Author of sin. He is without sin. He is the Most Holy. He abhors sin. Sin cannot approach Him. Sin cannot even set foot in the world of heaven, where He dwells. And now think you, that a God of such infinite holiness would lead men into sin? Would He compel them to do wrong by forcibly binding them in the inexorable chains of an evil destiny? Never. Hence we pronounce the doctrine of Fate a lie.

Again, if God Himself is the Author of sin, how can He command men not to sin? That He has given such a command, you yourselves admit. He has written that command upon the hearts of all men everywhere. If He is indeed the Author of sin; far from forbidding others to sin, He would take pleasure in their committing it. But He has, on the contrary, strictly forbidden it. This being so, we may unhesitatingly lay down the following principles, namely; that all sin is committed in direct opposition to the will of God, that God hates sin, and that it is impossible for Him to issue a decree of Fate binding men inevitably to its commission. Hence we conclude again, that the doctrine of Fate is a false doctrine.

Once more, if God is the Author of sin, how can He pronounce judgment upon sinful men? Hell is the fruit of wicked deeds. You yourselves allow, that God does punish sinners by turning them into hell. But how can He thus punish them, if He has Himself made a decree, which shuts them up unavoidably to the commission of sin? There could be no ground for His so doing. Yet nothing is more certain, than that the just God does punish sinners. Hence He is not the Author of sin. The doctrine of Fate is a pure lie.

Oh People! You are attempting to lay the sins, which you commit, upon God; and to effect this object you have craftily invented the doctrine of Fate. The attempt is utterly in vain. The sins, which you commit, are your own personal actions, not God's. Be alarmed then at your danger. Offer no longer the worthless excuse, that you sin because you are destined to sin. Consider this matter well. Will God, think you, accept your vain excuses? Will He overlook the blasphemy involved in them? Will He calmly endure the dishonor you put upon Him? Will He not rather plunge you, on these accounts, into a burning hell?

SECOND.

TO SAY THAT EVERY EVENT IS DETERMINED BY FATE IS EQUIVALENT TO SAYING, THAT MAN IS A MERE PUPPET DESTITUTE OF FREE AGENCY.

But this is plainly opposed to all the dictates of sound reason. Your own consciences bear witness, that men are not puppets. When the doing of a certain action is proposed to you; you unquestionably have the power either to perform that action, or to refrain from performing it, as you yourselves may choose. Suppose for example, that I tempt you saying, "Tell a lie for me, and I will give you a hundred Rupees." Coveting the money offered, you have, on the one hand, power to tell the lie, if you choose to tell it. Or reflecting that lies are sinful, you equally have, on the other hand, power not to tell it, if you so choose. The possession of this power proves conclusively, that you are not puppets, but free agents, endowed with the faculty of choosing and acting as you will. This is well known to you, your own consciences bearing witness to its truth. Hence the doctrine of Fate is a false doctrine.

Suppose a man, after coveting the money and telling the lie in violation of God's Law, should say, "That lie was not told by me, but was the result of inexorable Fate." Answer now for yourselves, whether you would accept such a statement as reasonable ? Would you not rather immediately pronounce it a bare-faced falsehood ?

Again, your actions also bear witness, that men are not puppets. Take the following as an illustration. A thief breaks into your house at night. You catch him, just as he is making off with your money, jewels and clothes. The thief addresses you thus : " My good friend ! You ought not to arrest me ; for this robbery is not my action at all, but the doing of that inevitable rogue called Fate. Fate is the culprit, not I. If you will but arrest Fate, drag it to the Police, and get it well punished, you will do an excellent thing. Fate is the most arrant thief upon earth. Secure Fate, and you will confer a priceless boon on the world. As for me, I am innocent ; therefore, kindly release me and let me be gone." Now what would you say to the entreating thief ? Would you not reply somewhat in this strain ? " You unprincipled villain ! Not only is there a divine command against stealing ; but you yourself know perfectly well, that robbery is a great sin. Notwithstanding this, you, in defiance both of God's law and your own conscience, have just broken into and robbed my house. And now that you are caught in the act, you begin to babble nonsense about the crime not being your's, but Fate's. One thing is clear, viz., that a rogue, who makes such excuses as you do, will never leave off stealing. A double punishment is what you richly deserve." And so saying, would you not forthwith drag him to the Police, and deliver him over to the officers of the law ? Undoubtedly you would ; and by this very act of consigning him to punishment, you would declare your full conviction, that men are not puppets, but free agents. Hence the doctrine of Fate is a false doctrine.

NALADIAR : 25TH CHAPTER : 8TH STANZA.

Literal Translation.

" That which makes a man stand firmly in a good station (or in good principles) is himself : that which makes a man

fall ruined from his station is himself: that which makes
a man rise steadily from station to station is himself: that
which makes a man reach pre-eminence is himself."

General Meaning.

In this verse, Nāladiar tells us, that a man's remaining fixed in a good position, and his falling ruined from
such a position depend equally upon himself. This
being so, men are not puppets; but free agents. Therefore again, the doctrine of Fate is a false doctrine.

THIRD.

YOUR ORDINARY EVERY DAY CONDUCT PROVES, THAT
YOU ARE NOT BELIEVERS IN THE DOCTRINE
OF FATE.

A boil has broken out upon your back. It is filled
with matter, and gives you intolerable pain. You know
no comfort by day, and get no sleep at night. Now
how do you act in such a case? Do you say, " Oh, this
is nothing but the result of Fate: let it have its course :
if this boil is to get well, it will get well; if not, it
wont: there is no use of my doing anything about it ?"
And do you so saying stoically bear the agony with
clenched teeth, seeking no relief? Not at all. You
apply fomentations. You smear the boil with ointments.
You swallow nauseous drugs. You observe a strict
diet. In short, you do everything you can to rid yourself of your pain. Hence it is clear, that you are not
believers in Fate.

Attend, while we give you another illustration.
You are the heads of households. The family must be
supported; wife and children are to be decently main-
tained. What course do you take? Do you say; "If
Fate has so decreed, I and my family will be supplied
with food and clothing; but if Fate has decreed otherwise, otherwise it must be: therefore there is no use
of my working for a support: all that I have to do is
to sleep, or squat idly in a corner of my house ?" Not
at all. You go out and work manfully. If you fail

to get a living in one kind of labor; you do not thereupon grow faint-hearted, but seek it in another. Nor do you cease your efforts, until you have provided bread for your own mouth, and the mouths of your children. Whence it is plain, that you are not believers in the doctrine of Fate.

Observe how Fate is driven before these arguments, like silk cotton before the July wind.

Oh People! You never assign Fate as an excuse in your worldly affairs. Why then do you make it a pretext for neglecting the interests of your souls? As a fowler lays his snares to catch and destroy little birds, so have the teachers of Fate laid a snare to ruin your souls. Go not near it. Let not your foot be caught in it. Destruction awaits all who become entangled in its toils.

Beloved! We now proceed to teach you the true doctrine concerning this matter; and to make it plain, we shall give it to you under four heads.

FIRST.

KNOW THAT GOD DIRECTS AND GOVERNS ALL EVENTS.

There is one only true God, the alone Possessor of infinite wisdom and infinite power. This God is above all and over all supreme. He both knows and foreordains every future event. Nothing happens without His will. All things whatsoever occur and eventuate in strict accordance with His purposes. He is the universal Lord.

SECOND.

KNOW THAT GOD HAS CREATED MAN NOT A PUPPET,

BUT A FREE AGENT.

A free agent is one, who has the power to do, or not to do a certain thing, as he may choose. Man is such a free agent. God has invested him with the power of approaching or of avoiding a certain thing; and of doing or of not doing a certain action, as he himself pleases. Hence man, though a creature of God, and existing only by

God's power, is still free, and no mere puppet.* It is because man is such a free agent, that God has given him a law. That law is briefly comprehended in the words, "Do not evil: Do good." If man is a puppet, how could this law be given to him? Such a law can be given only to those, who have power to do either good or evil, as they themselves may choose.

But perhaps some of you will here ask the question, "If God has thus fore-ordained, and if He thus directs all things according to His own will; is not man's freedom thereby destroyed?" We reply, No: for not only does God Himself declare, that He neither destroys nor impairs man's free agency; but our own hearts also bear witness, that we act with perfect freedom in doing many and various things every day of our lives. That God has decreed all events beforehand, and that He directs, controls and fulfils all things in accordance with His own decrees is perfectly true. Yet He never has put, and never will put men under any such restraint, as to destroy, or even to impair their freedom of action. He, who directs all things, directs them in such a way, as to leave man's liberty untrammelled. Carefully guarding that liberty, He yet accomplishes all the purposes of His sovereign pleasure.

This being so, no man has a right to say, "Since God orders all things as He wills, I am destitute of individual power and need do nothing." God has ordained, that men shall have oil. But to obtain that oil, man must himself gather sesamum seed and grind it in the oil-press. Otherwise he gets no oil. Hence it is plain that no one has a right to idly forbear effort saying, "Nothing can come from my actions." We are all bound to trust in God, and to submit cheerfully to His will; but we are equally bound to make strenuous efforts for our own good. And if we do our duty faithfully in both these respects, we shall find all, that God has decreed, working together for our good, and for His glory.

* See Appendix, page 150.

THIRD.

KNOW THAT IF A MAN SIN, HE WILL GO TO HELL.

It is sheer madness to say, " Whether I do right, or whether I do wrong, it can matter nothing ; for if God has ordained that I shall get to heaven, I shall get there in any event." That God has fore-ordained all things is perfectly true. But will you any the less be ruined, on that account, if you choose to do what is wrong? Take the following as an illustration. Some one, seeing you just entering a tiger's den, cries out, " Don't go there, come away, come away, there is a tiger inside." To this friendly warning you calmly reply, "That does'nt matter at all. If Fate has decreed, that the tiger shall not catch me, I shall not be caught ;" and with that you boldly walk into the recesses of the cave. Tell us now, do you believe, that, in such a case, you would escape being torn to pieces by the fangs of the wild beast ? Of course you do not. The application is obvious. If you walk in the ways of sin, you will never see heaven ; but must inevitably fall into hell.

FOURTH.

KNOW THAT A MAN WILL GAIN THE SALVATION OF

HIS SOUL, IF HE SEEK IT IN THE WAY OF

GOD'S APPOINTMENT.

Success is never obtained by merely wishing for success. To secure any good whatsoever, it is necessary that we both seek, and strenuously labor for its attainment. " Deer never go and fall into the mouth of a sleeping lion."* So if you do not seek your soul's good, your soul's good you will never find.

You know the proverb,

" The industrious man can never be disgraced."

* See Appendix, page 150.

M

Hear also what one of your poets says :

PATTANATTU PILLAI.

Literal Translation.

" Is there any good to be obtained without exertion ? Is there any evil, which may not spring from indolence ?"

General Meaning.

Here Pattanattu Pillai tells us, that all good comes from exertion ; and that all evil comes from indolence.

If a man ploughs, and digs, and hedges, and removes stones, and makes beds, and sows, and waters, and weeds, and drives away birds, and reaps, and brings to the house, he gets grain ; otherwise he gets none. In like manner, if we enter the way of salvation which God has pointed out, and diligently make the efforts which He has commanded, we shall obtain heaven ; otherwise we must fall into hell.

If now you inquire, " How are we to seek the salvation of our souls ; and where is the road that leads to heaven ?" we reply, that God Himself has answered these questions plainly in His Holy Word. Listen while we briefly explain this matter to you. There is not one sinless man upon earth. Some adore false gods ; this is sin. Some worship idols ; this also is sin. Some commit adultery and other impurities ; this also is sin. Some practice deceit, fraud, and theft ; this also is sin. Some tell lies ; this also is sin. We have all sinned. There is none righteous, no not one. Hence we all need a Saviour, a Saviour, who is able to expiate our sin, to redeem us from its fatal consequences, and to purify our polluted hearts. If there is such a Saviour, we can go to him, and through him obtain the salvation of our souls. He, who finds and believes on such a Saviour, has found the way which leads to heaven.

Beloved ! There is such a Saviour. That Saviour is Jesus Christ, the Son of God. He it is, who created all worlds, and who now sustains and governs the universe. How shall we attempt to tell His transcendent grace and love ? They are beyond the reach whether of speech or of thought ; inexpressible, inconceivable. This Jesus Christ, the only true God, descended to earth, and became incarnate as a man. To rescue fallen men, he appeared the Saviour of the world. While upon earth, He did many things, which none but God can do. He healed the sick with a word. He made the blind to see, the deaf to hear, the dumb to speak, the lame to walk, and the dead to live. By His voice, He controlled the winds and the sea. He knew and declared things hidden in the inmost recesses of human hearts. He pardoned sin. As when the Sun rises, light flows and covers the world; so, when Jesus Christ rose upon this earth, spiritual light and divine mercy flowed forth, and illumined its every part. He taught true wisdom, and pointed out to all men the way of salvation. He reproved the wicked. He bestowed heavenly bliss on those, who sought it at His hands. His teachings were all sweetness; His actions were all holiness; His gifts were all grace. After going about upon earth doing good for thirty-three years, He died for men. Nailed to the cross, He gave His life a ransom for their souls. His was no ordinary death. Words cannot express the terrible sufferings and the excruciating agonies he endured. On the third day after His death, He rose again alive from the tomb, and appeared once more upon earth. Then, after spending some days in animating and commanding and blessing His disciples, He left the world and ascended up to His home in Heaven.

Oh People ! The Lord Jesus Christ is the God who created us, and the divine Guru who procured merit in our behalf. The design of His sufferings was the expiation of our sins. Listen while we try to make this clear by an illustration.

Let us suppose, that you, after borrowing and recklessly squandering a thousand pagodas, find yourself utterly without means to discharge your enormous debt. Your creditor is inexorable. Your tears, your sobbings, your entreaties are all in vain. He will neither listen to, nor release you. " Pay every whit of your debt, or to cutcherry and prison you shall surely go ;" such is the only reply he gives to your pleadings. As you writhe terror-stricken at his relentless threats, a noble and generous prince, coming that way, sees your distress, and, his heart melting with pity, assumes your debt as his own. He knows that, by so doing, he must reduce himself to poverty ; yet regardless of his own interests, he sells his houses and property, gathers together all the proceeds, brings them, puts them in your creditor's hands, and thus redeems and saves you from his power. Would you not love that prince with all your heart ? Would you not proclaim his name and his generosity through all the towns and villages of the land ? Would you not teach your children to praise him ? Would you not obey his every behest ? -

Beloved ! Understand the meaning of this illustration. The sins we have committed against God are the debt, which we have incurred. If it remains unpaid, the punishment of hell is our certain doom. But to pay that debt we have not the smallest ability. The prince, who came to discharge it, is Jesus Christ. He, the sinless one, took the debt of our sins upon Himself as His own. He bore upon earth the punishment, which should have been inflicted upon us in hell. From the day of His nativity to the day of His death, He experienced sorrow and anguish in our behalf. It was to pay the debt of our sins, and to redeem us from eternal hell, that He died on the cross, and rose again from the dead.

Would you know whose debt of sin will be paid by Jesus Christ ? We reply, the debt only of those, who believe on Him, and walk according to his word. He will certainly save those, who trust in Him and adore Him as their Saviour. But all others will as certainly perish. Rejecting Christ as a Saviour, they can find no other way of expiation ; but must inevitably be plunged into the fiery lake of hell.

Oh People ! Reject utterly, from this hour, the false and pernicious doctrine of Fate.

If some one, seeing you walking in a dangerous and fatal path, should call out to you saying, " Oh Sir! don't go on in that path. It is the way to ruin. It leads into a dreadful wilderness, and ends in a deadly pit. Leave it at once, and come away ;" what, in such a case, would you do ? Would you saying, " As Fate has decreed, so must it be," go on in that path and die ? No. You would leave it at once, and turn into a good path. Do so in this case then. Relinquish at once the way of sin which is leading you down to hell, and enter upon the heavenly road which Christ has graciously opened before you.

Suppose again that, having fallen to the bottom of a deep pit, you find yourself sadly wounded and unable to move. What would you do in these circumstances ? Would you lie still with your mouth shut thinking, " Oh this is nothing but Fate ?" By no means. You would make all the noise you possibly could, crying out for some one to come and lift you to the surface. Dear Friends ! You have fallen into the pit of sin. Think then of Christ, and call aloud for His assistance; for He alone is able to lift you out of its depths, and bring you safely into heaven. If you cry out to Him with faith, He will surely give ear to your prayers.

Suppose once more, that you are alone battling with the waves of mid-ocean, and exposed to instant destruction. The sweeping gale ; billow after billow rising, foaming, roaring and beating upon you ; the shore out of sight far away in the distance ; all these things inspire you with unspeakable terror. But a ship comes near. Its captain throws you a rope, and calling out lovingly says, " Only catch hold, and I will draw you into the ship, and save you." What would you do in this case ? Would you refuse the proffered assistance ?

Would you reply, "Fate is irresistible. Let its decrees be fulfilled. I will not take hold of the rope." And so saying, would you calmly sink beneath the waves and die? No. You would at once eagerly seize the rope, mount up into the vessel, and cordially thank its captain for saving you from a watery grave. Beloved! You have fallen into the sea of sin. The merits of Jesus Christ are the only ship, that can cross its stormy waters. The Lord Jesus Christ is the captain, who alone is able to rescue sinners from its perilous waves. His Holy Word is the rope He casts within your reach. He calls out to you in tender accents saying, "Why will you perish? Oh sinner! Believe in my word. Come unto me, and through my merits you shall safely reach the shore of heaven." Lay hold then by faith upon this promise made by Jesus Christ. Come to Him with loving trusting hearts. Cast yourselves upon His merits, with a full assurance, that they will remove your sins, and bear up your sinking perishing souls. Do this, and you will certainly reach the heavenly shore, and enter into eternal bliss. .

APPENDIX to No. IX.

EXAMPLES AND ILLUSTRATIONS.

(1.) Men choose their own actions as freely as a potter chooses the shapes of the vessels, which he makes.

SANSCRIT SLOKA.

Literal Translation.

" As the maker makes what (vessels) he pleases from the clay-lump ; so man (acting as he pleases) reaps the fruit of the actions he performs."

General Meaning.

As a potter freely chooses what he shall fashion out of clay ; so man, freely chooses his own actions, and reaps the fruit of them.

(2.) Deer do not come, and fall of themselves into the mouths of sleeping lions.

SANSCRIT SLOKA.

Literal Translation.

" Undertakings succeed by means of exertion. They never succeed by desires. Deer do not enter the mouth of a sleeping lion."

General Meaning.

Deer never run into the mouth of an inactive sleeping lion, however hungry he may be. Undertakings are never accomplished through mere desire, unaccompanied by appropriate exertion.

SCRIPTURE TEXTS.

(1.)   God is not the Author of sin.
    Job 34. 10.
    Psalm 145. 17.
    James 1. 13.
    1 John 1. 5.

(2.)   God does not destroy man's free-agency.
    Deuteronomy 30. 15, 16, 19, 20.
    Joshua 24. 15.
    Proverbs 1. 10, 29 to 31.
    Isaiah 55. 1.
    Ezekiel 18. 23, 24, 31, 32.
    Ezekiel 33. 10 to 16.
    Isaiah 48. 18.
    Hosea 13. 9.
    John 5. 40.
    John 3. 19.

ADDRESS No. X.

IDOLATRY SINFUL.

OH People! You worship idols. We propose to show that such worship is treason against God, and a heinous sin. To do this, we shall set before you six propositions, and we ask you to give them your candid and attentive consideration.

FIRST.

THERE IS ONLY ONE GOD.

The following is what one of your poets says of His nature and attributes.

Literal Translation.

"Let us meditate on the all-pervading spirit, the fountain of bliss, the incomparable one, eternal, immaculate, incorporeal, free from disease, omnipresent, unalterably holy, distant and yet near, light dwelling in tranquillity, all-comprehensive, possessor of perfect felicity, pure intelligence inexpressible and inconceivable."

General Meaning.

This verse tells us, that God is eternal, holy, without form, perfect, omnipresent, the preserver, spiritual light, possessor of perfect felicity, the omniscient.

All this is true. God is just such a being as is here described. But do these attributes belong to the idols you worship? Is the image, which stands in your temple, eternal, holy, all-wise, omnipresent? No. Many of your own sages have taught the existence of a God, who is possessed of these exalted attributes. Why then do you, deserting Him, bow down to stones, which have not a single one of them?

Nitineri Vilakkam.

Literal Translation.

" What will not those affirm, who declare that a crow is white ? Some even say, that it is honorable to kill one's mother."

General Meaning.

What will they not say, who affirm that the crow is not black, but white ? There are not wanting some, who declare it an excellent deed even to kill one's own mother.

Absurd statements both of them you will allow; but neither of them so absurd as to say, that an idol is God.

Oh People ! When there is a God, possessed of all the most excellent attributes; how shall we characterize your leaving Him, and worshipping a stone as God ? Is it not sinful worship ?

SECOND.

God is a living God.

Why, leaving Him who has life, do you bow down to lifeless stones ? We know the common excuse you make for so doing. Your plea is, that life enters into the idol, when the Avāhana Mantra* is pronounced over it. The Brahmin especially, who recites that Mantra, is very strong on this point. He asserts positively, that, by the power of the Mantra, he gives life to the stone. But is it indeed true, that life enters into the idol ? Examine and see for yourselves. Everything that has life moves. Go where you may in this land, you see the image of Pillaiyār. If that image is really alive, it would sometimes stretch out its hand : it would occasionally plant its feet and walk : it would ever and anon swing its trunk. (The trunk of an elephant you know is never still). Or, as Pillaiyār has a good sized paunch, that at least would shake a little now and then. If life has

---

* The Avāhana Mantra is an incantation, by muttering which, the Brahmins say, they cause the deity to enter into images, thus rendering them proper objects of worship.

really entered his image, any or all of these movements would at times certainly occur. But they do not occur. Pillaiyār squats evermore motionless at the foot of some tree, or on the bund of some tank. The same is true of all the idols, which you worship. Lifeless and motion-less, they stay where you place them. Does any one of all the images you have set up with muttered incanta-tions ever come out and take a walk in the street ? No. They do come forth occasionally it is true ; but only when you yourselves place them on a frame, lift them on your shoulders, and with panting breath, and flowing perspiration, laboriously lug them about the streets. You construct immense cars for those idols. Did you ever see any of them climb up into those cars ? No. You yourselves lift them carefully into their places ; and you yourselves tie them fast with cords, lest they should fall. How in the face of all this you can say, that those images have life, we are at a loss to under-stand.

Again, you say that the Brahmin gives life to these images. But if the Brahmin really gives life to a stone ; why, when his child dies, does he not give life to that ? Why, covering his face with his hands, does he weep and utter cries of lamentation ? Surely he, who has made stones to live, ought to be able to revivify a dead child.

Once more, if the Brahmin really gives life to stones ; he must himself be God, for it is God's prerogative both to give and take away life. But if the Brahmin is God, how is it that he has to work and toil for a livelihood ? Would it be unlawful for him, who creates life, to create a little gold by way of appeasing his appetite ? Is it indeed indispensable, that one, who gives life to stones, must needs wander about from street to street, cheating peo-ple, and begging for a little rice, and a little tamarind, and a little ghee ? Giving life to a stone is certainly a majestic action ; but wandering about the streets beg-ging food looks to us a little shabby. The two things do not somehow or other, seem to accord. What then is the upshot of the matter ? Why just this, namely, that all this talk about giving life to stones is pure falsehood. An idol is always lifeless.

Hear what a poet of yours sings,

Translation.

" You call the planted stone a god, and adorn it with various flowers. Whence, sirrah ! the Mantra, with which you approach it muttering reverently ? Can the planted stone speak ? Is God in it ? Do the cooking-pan and ladle know the taste of the curry ?"*

Beloved ! God has graciously endowed you with life. Is it reasonable then, that you, who have life, should trust in a lifeless stone ? God has given you breath and speech. Is it right then, that you, who have breath and speech, should stand crying " Swāmi ! Swāmi !" before an image, which has neither the one nor the other ?

Oh People ! when there is a living God ; how shall we characterize your leaving Him, and worshipping a lifeless stone as God ? Is it not sinful worship ?

THIRD.

GOD IS THE CREATOR OF THE UNIVERSE.

He spread out the heavens above us. He formed the earth beneath us. He is the maker of all things visible and invisible. Why, leaving Him, who sits enthroned above all the Creator of the universe, do you worship worthless images ? If the image really made you, you ought of course to adore it. But far from its making you, you yourselves made it. When that image was a mere stone in its natural state, it was without eyes or mouth or nose or any other members. You yourselves were the cause of its getting all these. When it was destitute of eyes, you yourselves scooped them out for it. When it was without a mouth, you yourselves tore one open for it. When it was devoid of a nose, you yourselves made one protrude from its surface. Its

* See Appendix, page 163.

hands, its feet, its ears, and in short all its members were framed and fashioned by you. And after having yourselves thus given to it its form, you address it as a God. What strange infatuation is this? Since you made the image, the image ought to fall at your feet and worship you. Why then do you fall at its feet and worship it?

Tell us, you who bow down to stones! if those stones had a mouth that could speak, what would they say to you? Would they not reproach you with some such words as these; "Oh People! For what purpose did you come and seek us out upon our native mountains? Wherefore did you rudely pluck us thence, and loading us on carts bring us into the village? Why, treading on us with your feet, and rolling us over with your hands, and wounding us with your chisels, have you given us a form, and planted us in your temples, and shut us up in darkness?" A fit censure, could they only give it utterance. But you worship that, which has not a mouth to say even so much as this. If this be not madness, what is it? *

Oh People! when there is a God, who created you; how shall we characterize your leaving Him and worshipping as God the idols, which your own hands have made? Is it not sinful worship?

FOURTH.

God sustains and protects the universe.

He takes care of all that He has created. You yourselves are objects of His protection and providence. From your conception until now, He has unremittingly fed and nourished you. Even when, wrapped in profound sleep, you are unconscious of everything, you still breathe and live, sustained by His protecting mercy. Why, leaving the God who thus keeps and cares for you, do you prostrate yourselves before senseless idols?

The images you have set up do not protect you. They have not the power to protect even themselves. It is no uncommon occurrence, as you are all aware, for

* See Appendix, page 164.

robbers to break into your temples, and carry off the jewels, which adorn your idols. Surely it would be right for those idols to drive the robbers away, and protect themselves from spoliation. Why then do they not do so? Or if they lack ability to protect themselves, might they not at least give one good screech for help? But even this is beyond their power. The fact is, they are utterly incapable of protecting either themselves or others,

You yourselves are their protectors. You build houses for them, which you call temples. You yourselves carry them into those houses. You yourselves shut and lock the doors. You yourselves lug them out again. You yourselves lift them on your shoulders, carry them around the village, and, bringing them back, carefully deposit them in their places. The labor you undergo for them is not a little. Tell us now, did any of them ever make you so much as a salaam, by way of repaying you for your trouble?

The truth being, that you yourselves are the constant protectors of those idols; it is to us an unceasing wonder how the conception of their being your protecting deities ever originated in your minds.

Oh People! When there is an all-powerful God, who continually protects you by night and by day; how shall we characterize your leaving Him, and worshipping as God an image, of which you yourselves are the protectors?

FIFTH.

GOD IS THE BENEFACTOR OF THE UNIVERSE.

It is He, who makes the rain fall and fill your tanks. It is He, who, sending forth His light and heat, covers your fields with luxuriant grain. It is He, who clothes and feeds you. It is He, who showers upon you the comforts and luxuries you enjoy. The daily blessings which He vouchsafes to you are so many as to baffle computation. Why, leaving the God who confers all

N

these favors upon you, do you bow down to carved images of wood and stone?

Your idols are incapable of shewing you the smallest favor. They can do no more than stay quietly in the places, where you yourselves carry and put them down. All the homage you render them is, "like tamarind fruit dissolved in the river," utterly vain and profitless.

We quote what one of your poets says of them.

Translation.

"Gods there are baked and unbaked; gods there are planted and unplanted; tied gods there are, can they loose their fastenings? All they can do is to lie where you put them."

You confer many favors on these images. You wash them with water. You scour them with acids. You tie on their clothes. You put garlands and jewels on them. You anoint them with fragrant oil. You adorn them with flowers. All these kindnesses you do to them; but they do not in turn a solitary kindness to you. Are they your gods then, or are you their gods? Reflect and answer the question.

Oh People! When there is a God, who bestows numberless benefits upon you every day of your lives; how shall we characterize your leaving Him, and worshipping as God a carved image, which never has and never can confer upon you a single favor? Is it not sinful worship?

SIXTH.
GOD IS THE PUNISHER OF SIN.

He blesses those, who walk in accordance with His will. He punishes those, who walk contrary to His will. Why, leaving Him whom all are bound to worship with reverential awe, do you tremblingly offer supplications to stocks and stones?

Your idols are incapable of inflicting any punishment whatsoever. They cannot punish even the bats, which mute upon them, and make the room they occupy offensive. They cannot punish even the rats, which climbing up their faces in search of ghee, lick and cover, them over with spittle. They cannot punish even the dogs, which, without either shame or fear, publicly defile their persons. How then can these images, which are powerless to punish offending dogs, and bats, and little rats, punish grown up men like you? What possible ground can there be for your being afraid of them?

Oh People! When there is a God, Almighty both to save and to destroy; how shall we characterize your leaving Him, and worshipping as God a lifeless stock, which is powerless to inflict even the smallest penalty? Is it not sinful worship?

Beloved! In what respect do the stones placed in your temples differ from other stones lying about upon the earth's surface? In none. May we then worship all the stones, which we see scattered about everywhere, in the streets and in the fields, on the mountains and in the valleys? No, we may not. And just so you may not worship the stones, which occupy your temples.

We quote again from one of your sages.

Literal Translation.

"You break a sounding stone, and make idols of it. The stone, that forms your door-step, you tread upon and wear away with your feet: the stone, which is worshipped, you adorn with flowers and sacred ashes. Know that God takes delight in neither of these stones."

General Meaning.

You break a stone into two pieces. Placing one of them as a door-step in front of the house, you tread it beneath your feet; carrying the other to your temple, you set it up, bathe it with water, offer it flowers, and pronounce it to be a god. Know that the one piece is no more acceptable to God than the other. Both are stones and only stones. Such is the meaning of this verse.

Let stones be used for all the purposes to which God has appointed them. Let the washerman beat your soiled clothes on them. Let your women grind curry-stuff on them. Let your masons build them up into stone-walls. All this is right. God created stones for just such purposes as these, but you, diverting them from their natural uses, set them up and worship them under the pretext, that they are gods. Of all the follies prevalent upon earth, what folly is there greater than this ?

One of your poets sings as follows ;

Translation.

" Will the God of light, whose habitation is above all worlds, dwell in a broken image upon earth ? Will the Deity, who fills illimitable space, reside in contemptible stocks and stones ? Why, oh servants of the gods ! do you believe such ridiculous fables ? Heaven there is none either for those who tell, or for those who listen to them. If you will but devote yourselves to the divine Guru upon earth, you may dwell forever happy amid the changeless delights of heaven." *

Listen, while we recapitulate in brief the details of the foregoing pages. God is a real being. He is a living God. He is the Creator of all worlds. He is the Preserver of all things. He is the Benefactor of the universe. Him, and Him only should we adore and worship and praise. But an idol is a false being. It is destitute of life. It neither creates nor preserves anything. It can confer no good. It can inflict no injury. Leaving the true God, and worshipping idols is the folly of all follies. It is sinful worship. It is treason against God.

God has forbidden the worship of images. All those therefore, who bow down to wood and to stone, violate the divine law. They are despisers of God. They have reached the lowest deeps of the sea of sin.

God is a Spirit universal and everywhere present. As such, we are to apprehend and adore and worship Him with our hearts. To worship Him aright, we must first

See Appendix, page 164.

know Him aright. He is invisible to our bodily eyes. A true Veda is essential to a true knowledge of God. Such a Veda He has graciously bestowed upon men. The Christian Veda is the only true Sastra. It is to us instead of an eye. Without it, we are like blind men. If we read, and understand, and believe, and walk according to this Christian Veda, we shall know the true God. With the Holy Bible, as with an eye, we shall visibly behold Him. And thus beholding, we shall joyfully worship Him, who is a Spirit, in spirit and in truth.

God is an infinitely holy and just being. In Him there is no sin. But men are sinful souls. They have ruined themselves by the practice of lying, fraud, theft, idolatry and other crimes. They are enemies and traitors to God.

Because men have thus sinned, they are heirs of hell. Hell is their proper destiny, for their souls are defiled with sin. How then can those, who are thus sin-polluted and worthy only of hell, come into the presence of the Most Holy? How can they attain to heaven? There is but one way, and that is the removal of their sins. Thus and thus only can they approach God, and obtain eternal bliss. But men are utterly without power to remove their sins. They can find among themselves no way of escape from hell. They have no means of cleansing their guilty souls. What alas! shall they do? The punishment, to which they are hastening, is a never-ending punishment. Once in hell, all hope of escape is cut off for ever.

These things being so, a Mediator is required to stand between us and God. We need a Saviour, a heavenly Guru, who is able to expiate our sins, purify our souls, and bring us near to God. If such a one can be found; we, though ruined by sin, may through Him attain to holiness and to heaven.

If such a Mediator undertakes to remove our sins, He must Himself bear, in our stead, the penalty due to those sins. Otherwise our sins cannot be expiated.

God is a just God. He hates sin. He inflicts punishment for sin. Should He fail so to do, His justice would thereby be proved defective. The penalty He inflicts is a terrible penalty. It plunges sinners into the depths of hell. He, who would avert that penalty from us, must himself suffer its equivalent in our behalf.' If he does so, the justice of God will be satisfied. It will know no detriment. And thus the way will be open for God to pardon our sins.

Such a Mediator must have both a divine and a human nature. For if he be not man, how can he suffer for us; and if he be not God, how can he bear and carry away the fearful burden of men's sins? He, who would expiate our guilt, must be both God and man in the person of one all-meritorious Guru.

There is one only such Mediator. That Mediator is the Lord Jesus Christ. He is the true God. Yet He became incarnate as a man, and lived upon earth thirty-three years. He came as the Saviour of the world to remove our sins, cleanse us from impurity, and bring us unto God. While on earth, He taught true wisdom. He pointed out the way of life. He shewed mercy to all. He cured incurable diseases and distempers. He cast out devils. He averted calamities. He scattered blessings with a liberal hand. He did all these things by the simple power of His word. Thus while truly a man upon earth, He proved Himself, by many wonders and miracles, to be as truly God. He showed abundant reasons why the whole world should trust in Him and love Him as its Saviour. Finally, He gave Himself as a sacrifice for our sins. He was nailed to the cross. He shed His holy blood. He endured unspeakable suffering and anguish. He died. Rising again alive on the third day, He appeared to many on earth, blessed His disciples, and ascended up to heaven. Such was the divine work, which this glorious Mediator accomplished in our behalf.

Do you ask why Jesus Christ thus suffered and died ? Listen while we reply to your question. He took the burden of our sin, and carried it for us. That we might escape the eternal punishment of hell, He was punished in our stead. "But how is this," some of you will perhaps inquire, "was His human nature capable of bearing punishment equivalent to the eternal punishment of hell?" We answer, No, not of itself. If He were merely man, His nature would not have been equal to the task. But He was also God. His divine nature strengthened His human nature, in order that it might sustain the full weight of the penalty. It is by virtue of His being thus God and man in the same person, that He appears both fit and able to expiate our sins. The salvation effected by Jesus Christ avails for all, who believe on Him as their Saviour. It is confined to no one country; it is limited to no one nation. It is of world-wide application. All, of whatever land or tongue, who accept and love and follow Christ, are saved from falling into hell. That those who believe in Him might escape punishment, He was punished in their stead. He expiated their sins. To all such He gives His Holy Spirit. That Holy Spirit, dwelling in their hearts, makes them holy, and fits them to enter heaven. Thus they become the children of God, and will, at the moment of death, enter, through Christ, the world of bliss. There they will remain for ever happy in the presence of God.

Oh People! Cast away your worthless idols. Accept the Lord Jesus Christ, the all-powerful and all-loving Saviour of the world, as your God, your soul's friend, and your sin-destroyer. Embrace His holy religion. If you do so, you will by His grace attain to the transcendant joys of heaven. If not, you must inevitably fall into the flames of hell.

APPENDIX to No. X.

ILLUSTRATIONS AND EXAMPLES.

(1.) External religious observances are in themselves profitless.

PATTANATTU PILLAI.

Literal Translation.

" Religious rites and observances ; the Vedas and the Agamas ; morality and sacrifices ; offerings to the dead and daily worship ; prayers and incantations ; with the divine services, which men, having put on the Namam, or rubbed sandal and white ashes, perform at stated times every day : all these are worthless delusions."

General Meaning.

The abovementioned religious ceremonies and so forth are of no value.

(2.)   The worship of idols is extreme folly.

VEMANAR, 3 : 238.

Literal Translation.

" Oh Vemanar beloved of the gods ! What shall we say of those fools, who, having brought stones from the mountains, rolled them over with their hands and feet, and vexed them with masons' tools, afterwards bow down to those unpolished blocks ?"

General Meaning.

How shall we describe the folly of those, who bringing stones from the mountains, roll them over with their hands, tread upon them with their feet, cut them with chisels, and then bow down and worship them as gods ?

(3.)   A resolution to forsake idolatry.

PATTANATTU PILLAI.

Literal Translation.

" No longer will I adore chiselled stones, nor plastered images fashioned to resemble the Deity, nor copper idols polished with acids. I have clearly demonstrated, that true worship consists in fixing firmly in one's mind the two feet (of the divine Being) which glitter like fine gold. (Therefore) I desire nothing more."

General Meaning.

Idolatry is not worship. Heart worship alone is true worship.

SCRIPTURE TEXTS.

(1.)   Idols are not gods.

     Psalm 115. 4 to 8.   Psalm 135. 15 to 18.
     Isaiah 44. 9 to 20.   Isaiah 46. 1 to 8.
     Jeremiah 10. 14.   Jeremiah 51. 17, 18.
     Habakkuk 2. 18, 19.

(2.)   God forbids the worship of idols.

     Exodus 20. 4 to 6, 23.   Leviticus 19. 4.
     Leviticus 26. 1.   Deuteronomy 16. 22.

ADDRESS No. XI.

~~~~~~~~

IDOLATRY RUINOUS.

OH People ! You make many idols of wood and of stone and of clay, and offer to those idols various forms of worship. It requires only a little reflection on your part to convince you, that all such worship is ruinous Listen then, while we place the following arguments before you.

FIRST.

THE WORSHIP OF IDOLS IS A GREAT FOLLY.

You say that, because God is invisible, you, by way of helping your devotions, make and set up a visible image resembling Him. But what true knowledge can you gain by looking at the images, which you thus set up and worship ? Suppose you gaze ever so often at the likeness of some man, do you thereby become acquainted with that man's history and circumstances ? Can you, by merely looking upon his form, learn the village in which he was born, or the place where he was brought up ? Can you, by inspecting his image, ascertain what are his dispositions, and what his conduct ? His wisdom, his power, his office, his reputation ; will any of these become known to you by contemplating his likeness ? Never. No amount of looking or gazing, though you kept it up with both your eyes incessantly for a thousand years together, would afford you any real information concerning him. In like manner, it is evident, that no true knowledge of God can be acquired either by gazing upon or worshipping the idols, which you have invented.

Reflect further. Suppose that a man, whose form or image you had never seen, should clearly write his history from beginning to end in a book, and send it to you. Would you not, by reading that book, become acquainted with his birth-place and residence, his disposition and conduct, his intelligence and ability, his office and his rank ? You would. Just so, if God Himself should cause all that we need know concerning Him to be written in a Sastra, and given to us; we could undoubtedly gain a true knowledge of Him, by piously and attentively reading that Sastra. This being so, need we tell you, that the setting up and worshipping of images, without once inquiring for the true Sastra, which God has given concerning Himself, is an extreme folly ?

Again, it is sheer nonsense to say, that the idols which you make and set up, are resemblances of God. You have never seen God. How then can you fashion an image, that shall be like Him ? Certainly no one is capable of making a likeness of that, which he has never beheld. The idols, which you have made and planted all over the land, are many and various. But which one of them all will you venture to say resembles God ? Take Pillaiyār for example, whom you worship with so much veneration. Is his image a correct likeness of the Deity ? Has the Creator of heaven and earth really got, like that misshapen idol, a broken tusk, an elephant's trunk, and a swelled belly ? And does He keep a bandycoote for a vehicle ? Answer these questions for yourselves.

All you say, on this subject, is said without consideration. God is a pure spirit, and has no form. How then can an image be made of Him, who is formless ? It is a simple impossibility. Let us illustrate this by an example.

Some years ago, there lived in a certain village of the South country a goldsmith, who was a manufacturer of idols. He was a very clever workman, and employed himself in making and selling all sorts of images and statues. Learning this, a gentleman, who lived there, sent for the goldsmith, and on his arrival addressed him as follows, "Oh Goldsmith ! your reputation has reached even to me. I am informed, that you are a maker of images, which resemble God. Now I want you to make an image for me. All the gold needed for the purpose shall be furnished without stint. As to pay, we need say nothing about that. Whatever you ask I will gladly give. My only stipulation is, that you must make the image, exactly to a hair, like the pattern I show you. Do you agree to this?" The goldsmith replied; "I agree, Sir! I will make you an image differing in no respect from the model shewn me." Thereupon the gentleman, having named a day for him to come and begin the work, dismissed him politely. On the appointed day, the goldsmith came, bringing his tools. The gentleman requested him to be seated, and then, sitting down himself directly in front of him, spoke as follows, "Oh Goldsmith! You agreed to make me an image exactly like a pattern, which I was to set before you. Now stretch your eyes wide open, and take a good look at me. I want you to make an image of the soul, which lives in my body. Do it, and you shall have as many thousand pagodas as you ask for." On hearing this, the goldsmith astonished and bewildered sprung from his seat, and clapping his hand to his mouth exclaimed, "Alas Sir! what strange thing is this you require of me? Have I ever seen your soul? Can I ever see it? Is it not without form? No one is capable of making an image of the soul. Kindly dismiss me, Sir, and I will be gone." To this the gentleman replied; "Oh Goldsmith! I am seated in front of you, and am plainly visible to your eyes. Yet you confess yourself unable to make an image resembling the soul, which is within me. God never has, and never will be visible to your mortal eyes. How then do you dare to say, that the idols you make are like unto Him?" Offering no reply to this question, the goldsmith went away ashamed, and confounded.

TAYUMANAVAR.

Literal Translation.

"Oh Lord! Oh God! To nothing whatever will I (venture to) compare Thee, (lest I be) like those, who offer grass for sale in a shop filled with exquisite flowers."

General Meaning.

Oh God! There exists nothing to which I can compare Thee, and say, "Thou art like unto this." Should I venture the hopeless effort; my folly would be conspicuous as the folly of those, who try to sell common grass in a shop filled with resplendent flowers.

Oh People! Making and adoring images is folly. Idol-worship renders men fools. Is it not then pernicious? Is it not ruinous?

SECOND.

No good whatever results from the worship of idols.

It cannot allay the hungering and thirsting of our souls.

God and the human soul are distinct and separate existences. God is the Creator; and the human soul is the product of His creative power. Our soul is not one substance with God, nor will it ever become so. Yet if our soul, obtaining God's favor, gains admittance to His love, it will enter into eternal felicity, and dwell for ever prosperous and happy in His blissful presence. This is heaven. This is what we all need, and what we all long for. Our soul being of such a nature, it is plainly capable of feeling and exercising desires after God. He is our Heavenly Father. True we have left Him, and wandered far away in the paths of sin. Yet the desire to return to our Heavenly Father, and to enter into His celestial mansion has not entirely left our hearts. The wish to know God, obtain His favor, and gain admittance to heaven still lingers in our breasts. That wish is the hungering and thirsting of the soul.

TAYUMANAVAR.

Literal Translation.

"My thirst will never be quenched, until I quaff with my lips the sea of inexpressible felicity."

o

General Meaning.

The burning thirst of the soul can never be allayed, until it drinks of God, who is the ocean of unutterable bliss.

This is true. The cravings of a pious soul can be quenched only in God. If we do not obtain God, we must remain for ever unsatisfied. If we do obtain Him, our desires will at once be fulfilled. Our souls will be in a transport of bliss. This and this alone is true felicity. Will the worship of idols bestow this felicity upon us? Can our longings after God find their fulfilment in wood and stone? Can a misshapen idol satisfy the hunger and thirst of our souls? Never. Your idols are, as Tayumanavar says,

"Like the sand, which children boil as a substitute for rice in their play."

Little children playing in the street often make a fire-place of pebbles, and put upon it a small pot filled with sand, which they call their rice. Can that sand-rice appease their hunger? No. On the contrary, it would, if they ate it, give them the stomach-ache, and produce disease. When they wish to appease their hunger, they must leave that sand-rice, and going into the house ask their mothers for real rice. Now all worship of idols is like eating sand-rice. Far from relieving the soul's hunger, it only destroys the soul. Therefore renouncing it altogether, we must go to the true God, who is more loving than the best of mothers.

Again, Idol-worship will not help men in time of their calamity.

You must hereafter render an account to God of the sins, which you have committed in this world. God has appointed a day for this purpose. In that day, He will sit in judgment upon all the actions of your lifetime. Think you, that you will then dare to say; "Oh Lord! we worshipped idols, and by so doing our sins are all expiated?" No. Far from this, you will then learn, that your idolatry was a great sin, and that, in consequence of that sin, you are to be turned into eternal hell. Do you imagine, that the worship you rendered to idols while on earth will help you in that time of dire calamity? Alas! No. Instead of helping, it will only crowd and crush you into a deeper perdition.

One of your poets well asks;

"Can aerial flowers, or the mirage afford assistance in a time of need?"

There are no such things as aerial flowers. The mirage, which, in sandy wastes, has the appearance of water, is not water. Far from giving relief, it only lures on to destruction. The parched traveller who, believing it to be water, wearily drags himself toward it, gets no relief, but faints and falls and dies. In like manner idol-worship, far from saving you in the hour of calamity, will only deceive and utterly ruin you.

Understand then, that no good can come from worshipping idols. As one, who mistakes for teats the fleshy pendants hanging from the throat of a he-goat, gets no milk by seizing and drawing them; so he, who worships an image supposing it to be God, derives therefrom no good whatsoever.*

Oh People! Idol-worship not only confers no good, but also cuts you off from many and great blessings. Is it not then pernicious? Is it not ruinous?

THIRD.

IDOLATRY IS A FRUITFUL SOURCE OF EVIL.

It blinds the understanding.

If one ties a bandage so tightly over his eyes, that no light can enter them; he will, like a blind man who cannot see his way, grope and stumble and fall into the ditch. So long as he keeps the bandage on, he is blind. Idolatry is the bandage, which shuts and blinds the eye of the understanding. A worshipper of images,

* See Appendix, pages 177, 178.

unable to see the way to heaven, goes staggering and stumbling along the road to ruin. He must pluck off that bandage, and, flinging it aside, seek a good path, or he will inevitably fall into the pit of hell. Oh Ye, who bow down to idols! Ye are the blindest of the blind. The worship you offer is itself your blindness. So long as you continue to offer that worship; the light of the true Veda can never illumine your hearts, and you can never know the true God.

Any one may see at a glance, that the intelligence of the people, in this country, has been greatly blunted, not to say destroyed, by the worship of idols. When they see a lifeless bull carved out of stone, they do it homage with clasped hands. When they see a living moving bull, they hitch it to a cart, flog it, goad it, twist its tail, and drive it along before them.* Judge now for yourselves how blind must be that understanding, which, while it flogs the living animal, worships at the same time its lifeless image. Is not a worship, which thus blinds the understanding, pernicious? Is it not ruinous?

Idolatry ruins the soul.

The true God is the fountain of all blessings. The soul, which fastens itself on Him, will flourish and bloom with joy. But the soul, which leaving Him attaches itself to idols, must wither and die. Evil desires throng and gain strength in such a soul; while all sorts of wickedness flow forth from it, as from a tainted fountain. Such a soul loses all good, and gains all evil. As the body of a man, who rejecting food eats poison, dies and becomes food for worms; so the soul of him, who renouncing God betakes himself to idols, must perish, and become a prey to the flames of hell.† Is not this worship then, which thus destroys the soul, pernicious? Is it not ruinous?

Idolatry provokes God to anger.

A gentleman had a servant. The gentleman was a

---

* See Appendix, page 178.

† See Appendix, page 178.

good master, and paid the servant ten Rupees a month regularly and promptly. Whenever the servant received his wages, he was accustomed to make his master a grateful salaam. One day however, on being paid as usual, he neither salaamed, nor so much as said a word to him; but going out selected a stone, and carved upon it eyes, mouth, nose, ears and other members. Then setting it up in a corner of his house, he made it a salaam, and spoke as follows : " Oh Stone ! Art thou well ? Thou art my lord and master. Thou gavest me these ten Rupees, which I hold in my hand. Thou providest for me and my family month by month. Therefore, Oh Stone ! I make salaams to thee." The gentleman, witnessing this transaction, became very angry and reproved the servant thus ; "You ungrateful wretch ! When you know that I am your master, and that it is I, who give you your wages; how do you dare to set up this stone, and call it your lord, and make salaams to it ?" On hearing this, the servant impudently, retorted ; "You are not my lord ; that stone alone is my lord and master. It is from its hand and no other, that I get my livelihood." Thereupon the gentleman, reflecting, that if he kept this man any longer, he would certainly corrupt the other servants, drove him in disgrace out of the premises. None will deny, that his thus getting angry and dismissing such a servant was perfectly reasonable. Oh People ! God is our only Lord and Master. It is He, who sustains and protects us. It is He, who feeds and clothes us. It is He, who bestows upon us every blessing and comfort that we receive. If you, wantonly and ungratefully leaving Him, set up and worship a stone as God, He will certainly be angry with you and turn you into hell.

If you had conducted yourselves in such a way as to excite the anger of an earthly monarch, you would be greatly alarmed and terrified. You would tremble at the thought, that he might put you in chains and in prison, or make you carry dirt on the roads, or condemn you perhaps to the gallows. Now if you are so much afraid of an earthly king, who is no more than a man like yourselves ; how is it that you venture to act so defiantly and rebelliously towards God your Creator, who is the King of kings ? You might perhaps, by some means or other, escape the wrath of an earthly prince, and avoid the penalties he threatens to inflict. But how can you escape from the anger of the Omnipresent and Omnipotent God ? Oh People ! Is not idolatry, which thus provokes God to anger, pernicious ? Is it not ruinous ?

Idolatry results in the eternal loss of the soul.

ANONYMOUS STANZA.

Literal Translation.

" Men, ignorant of the transcendent perfections of the great God, worship every object they see, under the delusion that it is a heaven-conferring divinity. Vainly imagining such worship to be a sacred law of antiquity, they, by practising it, lose heaven and fall into a burning hell."

General Meaning.

Ignorant of the exalted attributes pertaining to the invisible God, men worship visible images as gods. Deluding themselves with the belief, that such worship is right, they madly forfeit heaven, and plunge into eternal hell.

Many other of your sages also have borne a similar testimony. We cite one example more.

ANONYMOUS STANZA.

Literal Translation.

" However many the stones you worship, Oh foolish Ones ! think you, that you will get heaven thereby ? Bathe yourselves thoroughly, and practice what austerities you may ; will they procure for you unutterable bliss ? Oh Madmen ! Purchasing stones with money, you call them gods and bind them in cloths. Do you imagine that, by so doing, you will after death enter Kailasa ? You will not ; but will fall into dreadful hell."

Oh People! Is not Idolatry, which thus plunges the soul into hell, pernicious ? Is it not ruinous ?

Suppose you had to cross the foaming torrent of a large and flooded river ; would you, instead of getting on a raft, plunge into the stream, carrying a grindstone by way of a support ? If you did ; would the grindstone keep you afloat, or would it drag you to the bottom of the river and kill you ? Oh People ! We all need to cross the river of sin. The divine Guru Jesus Christ is the raft provided for us. If rejecting His assistance, you attempt to cross with the help of your stone gods ; you will never reach the shore of heaven, but will be dragged down and hopelessly fixed in the depths of hell.

Beloved ! Cast away as false and worthless the idols, which can afford you no help, and seek at once the divine Guru, who is in every way qualified to save you. Know Him, believe in Him, attach yourselves to Him, and thus through Him reach the shore of heaven. There is one only such Guru. His name is the Lord Jesus Christ. He is the Friend of the soul, and the Destroyer of sin. He is the Sovereign of the Universe, the only true and living God. From the love He bore to us, He descended to earth, and became incarnate as a man. He came as a good Shepherd to seek and to save us, who are wandering like lost sheep in this wilderness world. His majesty and grace transcend all powers of description. While incarnate upon earth, His holy mouth gave utterance to the sweet words of true knowledge. He shone a pattern of unsullied holiness. He effected the removal of sin, and opened the way to heaven. He clearly manifested His divine power. He alone is the celestial Guru. He alone is the High Priest of the world. He alone is the heavenly King, fitted to rule and nourish and guide our souls. He showered mercies upon all, who sought His gracious assistance. By His all-powerful word, the blind saw, the deaf heard, the dumb spake, and the lame walked ; while devils and fiends fled, unable to endure the majesty of His presence.

This Jesus Christ, whose glory infinitely transcends our reach of thought, underwent great poverty and humiliation for us. For us, He suffered cruel persecutions and a terrible death. If you would know why, listen earnestly, while we unfold the reasons to you.

All men have the bitter consciousness, that they are sinners. Should any venture to declare himself sinless, who would believe his declaration? Do not men tell lies? Do they not deceive? Do they not give way to anger, hatred, envy, malice, and the like? Do they not fondly cherish these wicked dispositions? Do they not use foul language? Do they not pratice obscene actions? Thus they have become utterly corrupt in thought, in word, and in deed. Nothing is more certain than that all men are sinners.

We cannot of ourselves expiate the sins we have committed. We cannot save ourselves from the result of those sins, which is eternal hell. We cannot procure for ourselves the bliss of heaven. Hence all men in all lands agree in acknowledging the need of a sacrifice to remove sin. This is a good and proper acknowledgment. Such an expiatory sacrifice is indispensable to us all.

The Lord Jesus Christ has offered Himself up as such a sacrifice to remove our sins. The humiliation He experienced, the persecutions He underwent, the death He suffered, all had this one end in view. He bore the burden, which we should have carried. He, who knew no sin, assumed our sins as His own, and Himself endured the penalties due only to us. To remove our guilt, He gave His life for us on the cross. The anguish and the death, which He suffered, while hanging nailed through His hands and His feet to that cross, constitute the true and only sacrifice for sin. On the third day, He rose again alive from the tomb, appeared with glory upon the earth, commanded His disciples to proclaim His Holy Word in all lands, and then ascended up through the air to heaven. From that day to this, His servants have been preaching His love all over the earth, and inviting men everywhere to accept the way of salvation procured for them by the sacrifice, which He offered for their sins. The people of many lands, believing the gracious message, have accepted Him as their God, their divine Guru, the Redeemer of the soul, the Saviour of the world. And now those good tidings have been sent to you also in this land.

Oh People! Reject not this holy instruction. Jesus Christ is the one only Saviour, who is able to remove your sins, rescue you from hell, and bring you to heaven.

Beloved! Renouncing idolatry with all other forms of sin, believe in Jesus Christ, and walk in the way, which He has pointed out to you. By so doing, you will escape hell, and gain the eternal joys of heaven.

APPENDIX TO No. XI.

ILLUSTRATIONS AND EXAMPLES.

(1) God will not dwell in the five metals, or in stone, wood, and the like.

VEMANAR 3. 45.

Literal Translation.

" Hear, Oh Vemanar, beloved of the Lord! The Supreme Spirit will not reveal himself in clay, or in the five metals, or in wood, or in stones, or on pictured walls, or in images."

General Meaning.

God dwells not in stone, wood, clay, and the like.

(2) The worship of the Linga* is sinful.

PATTANATTU PILLAI.

Literal Translation.

" Fools, refusing to admit into their hearts the Spiritual Light, who, one and undivided, occupies and fills and pervades illustrious the eight cardinals with the sixteen intermediate

---

* The Linga is a phallus, which Saivaites worship as God. They wear it sometimes suspended from the neck; but more frequently tied on the arm a little above the elbow.

points and all other space, tie and bandage and fix Him beneath their armpits. Sinners are they all, mistaking midnight darkness for the broad light of day."

General Meaning.

Those, who worship the All-pervading God under a visible form, are sinners.

(3) Idolatry is utterly profitless.

VEMANAR 3 : 202.

Literal Translation.

" Hear, Oh Vemanar, beloved of the Lord ! Why, bringing blocks of marble, and building elegant temples, do you joyfully worship stones ? What do you gain by worshipping those stones ?"

General Meaning.

Why do you bring marble blocks, and build temples and rejoicingly worship stones ? What profits all this adoration of lifeless images ?

(4) Worshipping bulls made of stone, they ruthlessly beat living bulls.

VEMANAR 3 : 240.

Literal Translation.

" Hear, Oh Vemanar, beloved of the Lord ! Seeing a bull made of stone, men reverently bow down before it : seeing the living moving animal, they flog it. Looking into the matter, (we conclude that) all, who are pious towards bulls, are sinners."

General Meaning.

They worship the stone-bull, while they beat and torture the living one. Those, who believe in bulls, are great sinners.

(5) Ignorant souls who think, that God is in images of stone, clay, and the like, will not reach heaven.

SANSCRIT SLOKA.

Literal Translation.

" Fools who imagine, that God dwells in idols made of clay, stone, the five metals, wood and so forth, (vainly) practice painful austerities. They will not attain to supreme felicity."

General Meaning.

Vain are all the painful austerities of those, who stupidly imagine that God dwells in images of stone and wood and brass. They will never reach heaven.

Scripture Texts.

Idolatry blinds the understanding.

Romans 1. 21 to 32.

Idolatry provokes God to anger.

Deuteronomy 27. 14. 15. Isaiah 42. 17.
Jeremiah 1. 16. Jeremiah 8. 19.
2 Kings 22. 17. Psalm 78. 58, 59.
Revelations 21. 8.

ADDRESS No. XII.

CASTE.

OH People ! We propose to prove by many unanswerable arguments, that the distinctions of caste, which you so rigidly maintain, are all false.   Listen attentively then to what we here offer you.

You say, that there are four different castes.

JATI NUL : MANU URPATTI.

Literal Translation.

" Brahmins sprung from the face of the Swan-rider Brahma ; Kshattriyas with shining crowns from his shoulders; Vaisyas from his glorious thighs ; Sudras from his feet."

General Meaning.

This verse tells us, that Brahmins sprung from Brahma's face, Kshattriyas from his shoulders, Vaisyas from his thighs, and Sudras from his feet.   Most of your other Sastras also agree in affirming the same.*

If it is indeed true, that men were born in the way above indicated, we cannot at all understand how they can be, as you declare, of four different castes.   For if all men are the offspring of a single person, Brahma ; how can there possibly be four different castes among them ?   If a man has begotten four sons, can there be any distinction of caste among those children, all born of one father ?   Might we, looking at the four boys, say ; This one is a Brahmin, this a Kshattriya, this a Vaisya, and this a Sudra ?   The very idea is absurd.   Now you affirm that Brahmins, Kshattriyas, Vaisyas, and Sudras all have their origin from one and the same father, namely Brahma.   If this is true ; it follows, as a matter of course, that they are not of four castes ; but all of one and the same caste.

* See Appendix, page 196.

Look a little further into this matter. Can a difference of caste be detected among the fruit produced by any single tree? No. Take the Jack-tree as an example. Some of the fruit on this tree is, as you know, produced from its upper branches; some from the forks of its limbs; some from the middle of its trunk; and some from its foot close by the roots. Now is there, we ask, the slightest distinction of caste to be noted among these fruit, because they thus spring from four different parts of the tree? Would it be proper, looking at those fruit, to say; "That produced on the upper branches is Brahmin fruit, that in the forks is Kshattriya fruit, that on the middle of the trunk is Vaisya fruit, and that at the foot is Sudra fruit? Would not the whole world laugh scornfully at any one, who should venture to say so? Although the fruit is produced in four different places; yet, the whole being the offspring of a single tree, it is all plainly of one caste, and not of four. Now you say, that certain men sprung from Brahma's face, others from his shoulders, others from his thighs, and others from his feet. If this is true, we are at a loss to see how they can possibly be of four different castes. As all the fruit of a Jack-tree, though springing from four different places upon it, is of a single caste; so all men, if they are, as you say, the offspring of a single person Brahma, must likewise be of one and the same caste, even though they may have come from four different parts of his body. Hence it seems to us very strange, that you should declare them to be of four distinct castes.

But to let that pass; certain other of your Sastras give quite a different account of the origin of caste. For example:

16th B'HARATA VENPA: SANTI PARUVAM: ARAM URAITTA SARUKKAM.

Literal Translation.

"Oh King of kings! Oh Child, who cherishest virtue! Oh Prince, whose banner is inscribed with a drum! The distinctions of caste among men, who were in the beginning created by the lotus-dwelling Brahma, arose from their ornaments, their food, and their occupations."

General Meaning.

If you ask, Oh king! the origin of caste distinctions among men, who were in the beginning, created by Brahma ; learn that those distinctions arose solely from the various ornaments which they wore, and from the differing food which they ate, and from the diverse occupations in which they engaged.*

From this authority we gather three things, namely; 1st. That in the beginning, men were all of a single caste : 2nd. That subsequently they, by following their various tastes in dress, food and occupation, created distinctions among themselves ; and 3rd. That to the distinctions thus created they gave the name of caste.

Now mark well what we have here. One Sastra authoritatively informs us, that, "in the beginning, four distinct castes of men were created." Another Sastra as authoritatively says ; "Not so ; in the beginning all men were created of a single caste." Thus your Sastras, being at variance among themselves, are contradictory one of another. Is not this, of itself, sufficient evidence to prove, that those Sastras, far from having God for their author, are nothing but the cunning fabrications of artful men ?

If now you ask, which one of these two conflicting statements—namely, that men are of four distinct castes, and that they are of but one caste—is to be accepted as right ; we reply, that you may yourselves easily decide the question, by observing the condition of mankind throughout the world. Your doctrine is, that God Himself created and appointed all, who are teachers, to be of the Brahmin caste ; all, who are warriors, to be of the Kshattriya caste ; all, who are cultivators† of the

---

* See Appendix, page 196.

† There are three occupations set down as peculiar to the Vaisyas, viz., cultivation, merchandize, and keeping of cattle. Cultivation however, being the chief of them, we have mentioned it alone, as sufficient for our purpose.

soil, to be of the Vaisya caste; and all, engaged in other occupations, to be of the Sudra caste. If now it be true, as you say, that God.Himself has appointed those, who are engaged in these four different occupations, to be of four distinct castes, that divine appointment ought to hold equally good in all countries the world over. But it is not so. These four occupations are, as you well know, not confined to this land; but are followed by mankind in all countries whatsoever. Yet we do not find men, who are engaged in these four different pursuits in other lands, divided into four separate castes. There are China and many other countries inhabited by black races; and there are England and many other countries settled by white races. Look at them and judge for yourselves.

The abovementioned four occupations are carried on in all those countries, just as they are here. Yet in no one of them can we trace the smallest distinction of caste. Giving and receiving in marriage, food and drink, together with everything else, are in those lands common to all. The people of this country alone excepted, men engaged in those four pursuits are, all the world over, of a single caste, and not of four different castes. If God has indeed created men of four distinct castes, four distinct castes of men would undoubtedly be found in all other countries, as well as in this. But the case being entirely otherwise, as we have just seen, it is clear, that this four-fold distinction of caste, far from being of divine appointment, is only a fraudulent device of the people of this land.

Kapila, your great Muni, says the same. We quote from him the following verse.

KAPILA.

Literal Translation.

" In the numerous countries* inhabited by Ottiyar, Miléchchar, U'nar, Singalar, Chōnagar, Yavanar, and Chinattar, there are no Brahmins. Oh inhabitants of this land ! You yourselves have instituted the distinction of

* Countries bordering on India, north and south.

four castes, as though it were a law established at the creation of the world. High caste and low caste appear only in men's conduct."

General Meaning.

Brahminism is unknown among the Ottiyar, Milech-char, Unar, Singalese, Chōnagar, Yavanar, and the Chinese. You alone, who live in this country have established the distinction of four castes ; a distinction unknown at the time of creation., A man's conduct and manners alone shew whether he is of high, or of low caste. Such is the testimony of Kapila.

Oh People ! It is evident, that you have given but little thought to this matter. If it be really true, that four distinct castes of men were created by God ; differences, so plain as to be easily noted by all observ-ers, would certainly appear between persons belonging to the different castes. There are many kinds of beasts. There are many kinds of birds. There are many kinds of trees. The differences, existing among these, are too apparent to escape the most casual observers. Hence we naturally and properly divide them into various castes. But among men, it is far otherwise. Listen while we develope this matter a little.

You know the ox, the elephant, the horse, the lion, the tiger, and other beasts. Now there is a great dif-ference in the legs of these various animals. Each has a leg peculiar to its own kind. If required to pro-nounce upon their legs, we find no difficulty in distin-guishing them one from another. We are able at once to point and say ; This is the leg of an ox, that of an elephant, that of a horse, that of a lion, that of a tiger, and so on. The difference appears at the very first glance. Now it is because of this manifest difference in legs, that we speak of an ox species, an elephant species, a horse species, a lion species, a tiger species ; and thus naturally divide them off into many and various castes. But when, on the other hand, we look at Brahmins, Kshattriyas, Vaisyas, and Sudras, who you say belong to four entirely distinct castes ; do we discover any such marked difference in their legs? Is there any manifest dissimilarity or peculiarity whereby we may be led to decide and say; This is a Brahmin's leg, that a Kshattriya's, that a Vaisya's, and that a Sudra's? Nothing of the kind. Their legs are all of one and the same shape, undistinguishable. Hence we conclude, that the distinctions made between Brahmins, Kshattriyas, Vaisyas, and Sudras are false and ridiculous. They are not of four castes; but of one and only one caste.

Again, the ox, the buffalo, the horse, the elephant, the ass, the monkey, the sheep, the goat, and, in short, all kinds of animals are easily distinguished one from another in many other respects. For example, each species has a form, and a smell, and a voice peculiar to itself. But we discover no such peculiarities distinguishing Brahmins, Kshattriyas, Vaisyas and Sudras. You say, that they are of four different castes. But they all look alike, smell alike, and talk alike. Hence we again conclude, that they are of one, and not of four castes.

So Kapila also says in the stanza following:—

Literal Translation.

" Who has ever seen among men a difference in form, like the difference between an ox and a buffalo? No dissimilarity appears in their duration of life, their members, their bodies, their dispositions, or their intelligence."

General Meaning.

There are no such differences of form among men as exist between an ox and a buffalo. No dissimilarity can be detected in the duration of their lives, or in their members, or in their bodies, or in their dispositions, or in their intelligence.

Once more; the swan, the dove, the cuckoo, the parrot, the peacock and other birds differ widely from each other in their shapes, their colors, their feathers, their tails, and their beaks. But it is manifest, that there are no corresponding differences to be noted among

Brahmins, Kshattriyas, Vaisyas, and Sudras, who are falsely declared to be of four distinct castes. From the absence of such differences, they are all evidently of one, and not of four castes.

Look again at the varieties of trees. There is a banyan tree, a mango tree, a cocoanut tree, a palmyra tree, a makula tree, a coral tree, an Ashoca tree, a tamarind tree, a champac tree, &c., &c. These are all easily distinguished one from another. They differ in their roots, their trunks, their branches, their twigs, their leaves, their buds, their flowers, their fruits, their barks, their hearts, their seeds, their saps, and their odors. But we look in vain for any such marked difference as these among Brahmins, Kshattriyas, Vaisyas, and Sudras, whom you absurdly declare to be of four distinct castes. They do not differ at all either in their skins or their hair, their flesh or their blood, their bones or their brains, their color or their shape. They are all of the same kind. Therefore they are all of one, and not of four castes.

Observe yet another thing. Have the male and female of two different species of beasts ever been seen to unite, and generate offspring? Have a cock and a hen of two distinct kinds of birds ever been known to mate, and hatch young from their eggs ? Such a thing never occurred. Propagation cannot result from the union of different species. But how is it with regard to those of the human species, whom you affirm to be of four distinct castes ? Let the male and female belong to what caste they may; are not children born to them, if they marry and live together ? Yes. Hence it is beyond a doubt, that all mankind are of one and the same caste.

Many of your own sages have used this same argument against caste. We give you an example or two.

KAPILA.

Literal Translation.

" Oxen and buffaloes are by birth different from each other. Have the male and female of these two species ever been seen to unite and breed ? Oh you, who affirm, that men are not all of one caste by birth ! Can it be, that you have never seen the males and females of those, who you say are of different castes, uniting with each other, and by that union procreating their young ?"

General Meaning.

Oxen and buffaloes being of distinct species, they have never been known to mate and produce young ; but all are aware, that children are constantly procreated by the union of men and women of the so-called different castes.

Gnāna Vettiyān argues in the same way.

GNANA VETTIYAN.

Literal Translation.

" If a goat cover a sheep, will young be produced ? If a buffalo cross with a cow, will a heifer be born ? Again ; let a man of your caste cohabit with a woman of my caste ; could you decide whether their child is of your caste or of mine ? Once more ; will eggs result from the mating of a common cock and a paddy-bird ? Will chickens come from the union of a heron with the ordinary hen ? Will a Churai-creeper spring from the seed of a Pallappāgal ?"

General Meaning,

Will young be produced by the union of a goat with a sheep, or of a buffalo with a cow ? If a barnyard cock mate with a paddy-bird, or a heron with a barnyard hen ; will chickens be generated ? Will a Churai-creeper spring from the seed of a Kulippāgal ? Let a male of my caste unite with a female of your caste ; could you tell to which of the two castes their children belong ? So reasons Gnāna Vettiyān.

Such marked differences being discernible among beasts, birds, and plants, they are, as we have said before, naturally and properly distinguished into various species or castes. But there are no such differences seen among men. Hence the entire human race are of but one and the same caste.

Again ; if we regard the way in which all men are born, the way in which they live, the way in which they die, the way in which they move their hands, feet, tongues and other members, the way in which they exercise their minds and their wills, and the way in which they estimate objects of sense; if we notice the food they eat, the medicines they take, the joys and sorrows they experience; we find that all these are alike common to the Brahmin, the Kshattriya, the Vaisya and the Sudra. Hence all are of one caste, and not of four castes.

We quote once more from Kapila Muni.

KAPILA.

Literal Translation.

" Does the rain discard certain men when it falls ? Does the wind reject certain men when it blows ? Does the great earth say, l will not carry certain men ? Does the Sun say, I will not shine upon certain men ? Is the food of the higher castes (found) in the fields, and the food of the lower castes in the jungle ? (No. Therefore), for all the human race, there is but one caste and one lineage, one death and one birth."

General Meaning.

Does the rain fall upon some men, and not upon others ? Does the wind blow for some men, and not for others ? Does the earth maintain some men, and refuse to maintain others ? Does the Sun shine upon some men, and leave others in darkness ? Are the higher castes fed by the cultivated fields, and the lower castes by the jungles ? Nothing of the sort. Therefore it is evident, that all men in all lands are of but one caste and one lineage. In birth and in death they are alike undistinguishable.

Again, several of your sages have taught, that men can properly be distinguished into only two castes ; viz., one embracing all the good, and the other all the evil.

NALLA PILLAI B'HARATA : ATI PARUVAM :
VARANAVATHAI SARUKKAM.

Literal Translation.

" Learned men, beautiful maidens, liberal handed persons, valorous warriors, prosperous kings, and ascetics, who are true and faultless sages, are all of one caste. There is no distinction into high and low."

General Meaning.

Learned men, excellent maidens, open-handed persons, heroes, monarchs, and Rishis are all of one and the same caste. Hence all pretended distinctions of high and of low caste are false and non-existent. So says the Maha B'harata.

NALADIAR: 20th CHAPTER: 5th STANZA.

Literal Translation.

"The terms high caste and low caste are mere words without substance. Abundant ancestral wealth, religious austerities, learning, energy; these are what make caste."

General Meaning.

The Naladiar here tells us, that the terms high caste and low caste are mere words devoid of meaning: and that true caste has its origin only from wealth, asceticism, erudition, or active industry.

NALVALI.

Literal Translation.

"There are two castes, and no more. Those upon earth, who give according to the established rules of undeviating virtue, are high caste: those, who do not give, are low caste. This is the testimony of the Vedas."

General Meaning.

There exist two and only two castes. All, who lead a moral life, and give liberally to the poor, are of high caste; while those, who do not thus give to the needy, are of low caste. So says Avvyar in the Nalvali.*

Observe again the teaching of Vémanar.

"Call not him a Pariah, who was born a Pariah. It is not he, but the liar, who is the Pariah. The lowest of all Pariahs is one, who abuses a Pariah-born man, by calling him a Pariah."†

* See Appendix, page 197.

† See Appendix, page 197.

Oh People ! Weigh carefully the teaching of your sages contained in the verses we have just quoted. They tell you that all learned men, good women, liberal persons, heroes, righteous monarchs, sages, industrious men, and just persons are of high caste ; and that all illiterate, ungenerous, cowardly, unwise, and lazy persons, together with cheats, liars, and vilifiers are of low caste.

Beloved ! We desire to say a few more things to you about the distinctions of caste, which have been invented in this country. We ask you to give them a kindly hearing and a fair consideration.

FIRST.

Caste Distinctions are founded on Folly.

Vémanar writes as follows :*

" What virtue is there in food ? What merit in lineage ? What efficacy in natal soil ? It is ridiculous to see the sufferings men voluntarily endure in observance of their caste."

Listen also to Sūtar.

Sutar.

Literal Translation.

" Hear, Oh ye wise Munis who desire heaven ! The simpleton who, all unconscious of the true faculties of the soul, gives his whole mind to caste and lineage, will wander about like worthless chaff. Delirious pleasure will be his only reward."

General Meaning.

Oh Sages ! The fool, who, having no acquaintance with true spiritual knowledge, is wholly taken up with caste and lineage, is worthless as chaff. The only pleasure such a one can have is a phrensied intoxication.

SECOND.

Caste Distinctions have their origin
in Arrogance.

Brahmins and a few others like them, conceiving the purpose of exalting themselves and degrading every-

* See Appendix, page 198,

body else, have instituted the distinctions of high and low castes. Arrogantly placing themselves at the top, they carry a haughty front; and insolently trample, as it were, all others beneath their feet. Can a scheme so nefarious have its beginning in divine mercy? Never. It has sprung from nothing else than the vicious dispositions of haughty rebels against God. This being so; need we add, that it is evil and pernicious in the last degree?

THIRD.

CASTE DISTINCTIONS ARE A GREAT FRAUD.

The Brahmins, by proclaiming themselves to be of superior caste, trick and defraud numberless persons. In accordance with the old saying,

"Selecting his victims, he cheated them with words,"

they delude many by their high-sounding pretensions, and plunder them of their wealth. The settled purpose of these Brahmins is, that others shall labor, toil, sweat, and gather, only in order to give to them; and, in accordance with this purpose, they habitually threaten to curse every one, who refuses to give what they choose to demand.

Now why do they do all this? Is it not that, avoiding labor themselves, and robbing others of their property, they may, without toil nourish their own bellies, and live luxuriously upon other men's hard-earned gains?

Hear what Gnana Vettiyan says of their tricks.

GNANA VETTIYAN.

Literal Translation.

"With this design, they publicly recited the Vedas, as of universal authority. Their teachings are nothing but falsehoods, similar to those, which men, in all times and in all countries, habitually repeat, as handed down to them from their ancestors. Furthermore, Oh my Lord! They fabricated rules dividing men into Brahmins, Kshattriyas, Vaisyas, and Sudras, and defining the duties pertaining to each of these four castes. The precepts, laid down in their works, are all eminently mischievous tricks, devised and manufactured by themselves. Knowing their perfidy, I, Valluvan, have thus brought it to light."

General Meaning.

The declaration, that the distinction of men into Brahmins, Kshattriyas, Vaisyas, and Sudras, and the duties laid down as belonging to each of those four castes are of divine origin and authority, is a wicked and most pernicious deception. I, Valluvan, publicly denounce the great cheat, which I have detected.*

FOURTH.

The Observance of Caste Distinctions is a
great sin.

There is but one God, the Creator of the world and of all its human inhabitants. As all, in common, owe their being to this one heavenly Father, the bond of a common brotherhood ought to be felt and acknowledged by all. Every man is bound to love all other men, as members of the same family with himself. But caste is utterly at variance with this obligation. It ruthlessly cuts and abolishes the bonds of brotherhood and of mutual affection among men. It fills their breasts with hatred and animosity one against another. Are not they then great sinners, who teach and uphold the system of caste; a system, which, as we have just seen, excites enmity and strife between man and man?

Again, Brahmins and others have daringly sought to confirm this pernicious doctrine, by casting the responsibility of its origin upon God; and, with this end in view, they have invented an absurd fable to the effect, that the four castes sprung respectively from the face, the shoulders, the thighs, and the feet of Brahma. Thus skilfully laying their plans, they have contrived to ruin the people of this land, by craftily enveloping them in the meshes of the false and treacherous system of caste. Can any deny, that their so doing is a great sin?

* See Appendix, page 198.

Furthermore, as one lie naturally gives birth to many lies, and one delusion to many delusions ; the people of this country have, by degrees, sunk deeper and deeper into mental darkness and bewilderment. Not satisfied with four castes, they have invented new and minor distinctions, so numerous and complicated as to defy all attempts at computation or arrangement. A careful estimate of these facts cannot fail to convince every candid mind, that the system of caste is a wicked and pernicious system, opposed alike to the government of God, and to the welfare of men.

FIFTH.

ADHERENCE TO CASTE ENDS IN RUINING THE SOUL.

In the Mahābhārata we find the following statement ;

"The highest form of religious life is a strict observance of the rules of one's caste."

The meaning is, that man's paramount religious duty is conformity to the laws of his own caste. Many, trusting in this maxim, are ruined and fall into hell. Their mode of reasoning is this. "It matters not what sins we may commit. Conformity to caste is the one great virtue. That of itself suffices for our salvation. Our conduct, in other respects, is a thing of no consequence whatever." And thus arguing, they give themselves without restraint to the commission of sin. Deluded by the belief, that caste usages are the way to heaven, they neither desire nor seek any other way. Hence their souls can never find the true road to bliss. Their delusion effectually shuts them out of God's favour. Blindly following the ways of sin, they finally fall into eternal hell.

Oh People ! Your Caste is the chief obstacle to your entering the way to heaven. Hence it is, that its observance is so great a sin. Your adherence to caste is, in no respect, a virtue. On the contrary, the more rigidly you conform to its rules, the more sin you treasure up against yourselves. Have you not already accumulated enough of such treasure? How long will you madly cherish the delusion, that caste is right and good? Alas! it is only too certain, that it is the way to hell.

Oh People! Listen to a faithful statement of the case. There are only two castes in the sight of the true and omnipresent God. Of these, virtuous souls constitute the one, and sinful souls constitute the other. Virtuous souls dwell in heaven, the world where God's glory shines resplendent. In that world, there is no sin. But upon this earth, all have sinned. Falsehood, deceit, robbery, and adultery prevail in its every land. Hatred and envy, anger and malice, avarice and lust are found in its every quarter. There is not a virtuous person in its wide extent. All, without exception, have violated the laws of God, and become sinners.

This being so, of what avail is all this strife about high caste and low? Cease your vain and profitless contentions. Recognizing that you, in common with all men, belong to the sinful caste, inquire for the means of expiating your sins. Search for the road that leads to heaven, and help each other to find and enter into it. This is necessary. This and this alone is reasonable.

Beloved! As we are all sinners, we all require a meritorious Guru, who is qualified to remove our sins. Unless we find such a Guru, we can never enter into heaven, the abode of virtue; but must, at death, hopelessly fall into the flames of hell. There is such a Guru. Jesus Christ is the name He bears. He is the Lord of the world of virtue. Pitying our lost condition, He, the Most High God, issued forth from heaven, and descending to earth, became incarnate as a man. He is the one only true Guru, all-loving and all-powerful. In none of the three worlds is there any other, who is qualified to save us. While dwelling upon earth, He performed most wonderful deeds. He showered love and grace upon its people. He exposed false systems of religion. He taught the true way. His Word was the Word of God, and carried omnipotence in its sound. Blind men heard it, and saw. Deaf men heard it, and rejoiced in their restoration. Dumb men heard it, and praised Him with opened mouths. Sick men heard it, and exulted in renewed health. Devils heard it, and fled away affrighted.

Jesus Christ procured merit for us, who are destitute of all merit. If we obtain His merit, it will rescue us from falling into hell. That merit, like a key, will open to us the gates of heaven. This gracious Guru Himself bore our sins. On account of our sins it was, that He was fixed with nails to the cross. It was for us, that He suffered death upon the tree. The punishment He endured was a great and terrible punishment. Do you ask why He, who was Himself without sin, bore such a punishment? It is a good question, and we answer it with pleasure. Jesus Christ was thus punished, in order that we might not bear the eternal penalty of hell. We are the guilty ones. The punishment ought to have fallen upon us. But He, wishing to avert our punishment, and save us from hell, suffered that punishment in our stead. On the third day after His death, He rose again with life from the grave, appeared once more upon earth, commissioned His disciples, and then ascended up to heaven. The place to which He went is the world of merit. He and He alone is the merit-giving Guru. Whoever believes in Him, and walks according to his Word cannot perish. He cannot fall into hell. The sins of such a one will all be removed by the merits of this Guru. He will become pure in heart. He will attain to the eternal bliss of heaven.

'Oh People! Be not careless and unconcerned about this matter. This is your time and your opportunity. Improve the hour of mercy. Renounce at once all your sinful ways, reject all false systems of religion, abandon your vain distinctions of caste, accept Jesus Christ as your God and your merit-bestowing Guru, trust in Him alone, acknowledge His Bible as the only true Veda, enter into the Christian religion, which He has established for all, and thus prepare yourselves for the supreme felicities of heaven.

APPENDIX to No. XII.

ILLUSTRATIONS AND EXAMPLES.

(1.) The four castes sprung from four parts of Brahma.

B'HAGAVATAM: MAITTIREYAR VIDURARKU TATTUVAM URAITTA AD'HYAYAM.

Literal Translation.

"From his face pre-eminent sprung the wearers of the sacred cord ; from his shoulders came forth kings ; from his elegant thighs proceeded wealth-abounding merchants ; finally from his feet were born the hindermost."

General Meaning.

The four castes, viz., Brahmins, Kshattriyas, Vaisyas, and Sudras sprung respectively from the face, the shoulders, the thighs, and the feet of Brahma.

(2.) The same with the foregoing.

SANSCRIT SLOKA.

Literal Translation.

"To people the worlds, Brahmā created Brahmins, Kshattriyas, Vaisyas, and Sudras from his face, arms, thighs, and feet."

General Meaning.

To inhabit the earth, Brahma created Brahmins from his face, Kshattriyas from his arms, Vaisyas from his thighs, and Sudras from his feet.

(3.) Men, originally all of one caste, were subsequently divided into four castes, by reason of their occupations.

SANSCRIT SLOKA.

Literal Translation.

"Oh Ud'hishdra ! (Formerly) this whole world was of a single caste. The four castes originated from specialties of occupation."

General Meaning.

Oh King! In the beginning, all mankind were of the same caste. Afterwards, they were distinguished into four castes, according to the various occupations in which they were engaged.

(4.)   Brahmins are of higher caste than others.

NALLA PILLAI B'HARATA: ANUSASANIKA PARUVAM: B'UDEVAR MAHIMAI URAITTA SARUKKAM.

Literal Translation.

"The prevalence of royal justice is all owing to the religious austerities of Brahmins. The profusion of abounding lives is all the result of Brahminical virtue. The fall of precious rain is all attributable to the Brahmins' recitation of the four Vedas. Tell us then, are there upon earth any who are more exalted than the Brahmins?"

General Meaning.

There are none upon Earth so exalted as the Brahmins.

(5.)   Learned men are the highest caste.

VEMANAR 2: 128.

Literal Translation.

"Oh Vemanar, beloved of the Lord! What profit is there in wandering about ignorant as to which of the castes is the highest? The man of knowledge is of the highest caste."

General Meaning.

Why weary ourselves in unprofitable efforts to decide which caste is the most exalted? The man of science is of the highest caste.

(6.)   Not those who are born Pariahs; but liars, and abusers of Pariahs are Pariahs.

VEMANAR 2: 135.

Literal Translation.

"Oh Vemanar, beloved of the Lord! A Pariah is not a Pariah. He upon earth, who is always breaking his word is a Pariah; and he, who calls a Pariah a Pariah, is the greatest Pariah of all."

General Meaning.

Birth makes no man a Pariah. Falsehood does make men Pariahs. The meanest Pariah of all Pariahs is he, who calls a Pariah a Pariah.

(7.) It is laughable to observe what sufferings men will undergo for the sake of caste.

VEMANAR 3 : 218.

Literal Translation.

"Oh Vemanar, beloved of the Lord! What has food done? What has caste done? What has country done? The body is nothing but a block. When we consider the sufferings men endure, (for the sake of caste,) they are simply ridiculous."

General Meaning.

All the sufferings and inconveniences, which men bring on themselves by adherence to the rules of caste, are absurd and ridiculous.

(8.) Caste is all a Delusion.

PATTANATTU PILLAI.

Literal Translation.

"Oh God! Ignorant of the fact, that Thou didst create but one caste, I, dwelling in this vessel of filth, (i. e. the body) foolishly imagined (that there were many castes)."

General Meaning.

The idea, that all men are not of one and the same caste, is the merest delusion.

SCRIPTURE TEXTS.

Genesis 1. 27, 28.
Genesis 3. 20.
Genesis 9. 18, 19.
Malachi 2. 10.
Acts 17. 26.

ADDRESS No. XIII.

BRAHMINISM.

OH Brahmins ! You affirm, that the Brahmin caste is the highest of all castes. In the Sastras also, which are your own compositions, you have recorded similarly arrogant assertions about yourselves. We quote one here as an example.

ANONYMOUS STANZA.

Literal Translation.

" Listen, Oh sinless One ! while I relate the way, in which men became four castes. According to their deeds, (performed in previous births) they sprung joyfully from the feet, the thighs, the shoulders, and the face of the holy Brahma. Their (difference of caste) is owing to the difference of place (on Brahma's body, from which they were produced.) Those, who came from his feet, are the lowest ; while those, who sprung from his face, are the highest."

General Meaning.

In this verse, Siva addressing Parvati speaks as follows ; Listen, Oh Faultless One ! while I tell you how men came to be of four different castes. They were born from the feet, the thighs, the shoulders, and the face of Brahma. Their relative caste is decided by the particular part of that god, from which they were produced. Sudras, who came from his feet, are the lowest ; while Brahmins, who sprung from his face, are the most exalted.

The substance of this verse is, that certain persons are, by their very birth, Brahmins ; and that therefore they are superior in caste to all other men.*

* See Appendix, page 210.

We propose to demonstrate, in the clearest manner, that this is utterly false and erroneous. Listen attentively.

FIRST.

THE GREAT MUNI KAPILA TESTIFIES, THAT HIGH BIRTH IS NOT ESSENTIAL TO A MAN'S BECOMING A BRAHMIN.

KAPILA.

Literal Translation.

" Vasisht'ha who, like the red lily which springs from the mud, was born to Brahma from the womb of a concubine ; Satya, who was born to Vasisht'ha from the womb of a low-caste woman ; Parāsara, who was born to Satya from his union with a Pariah female ; and Vyāsa, who was born to Parāsara from the womb of a fisherwoman ; these four, reading the Vedas and becoming greatly renowned, shone as pre-eminent Rishis."

General Meaning.

The great sage, Vasisht'ha, was the child of a concubine. The great sage, Satya, was the child of a Pariah woman. The great sage, Parāsara, was the child also of a Pariah woman. The great sage, Vyāsa, was the child of a fisherwoman. Yet these four, made eminent by their study of the Vedas, became exalted Rishis. Such is the testimony of Kapila.

Not one of the above-mentioned great Rishis was born of a Brahmin woman. Their mothers were, as we have seen, respectively, a concubine, a Pariah, a Pariah, and a fisherwoman. Yet all acknowledge, that they were undeniably Brahmins. Hence it is plain, that mere birth is not the cause of Brahminhood ; and that, in point of fact, there is really nothing in lineage. This being so, the assertion, that any one becomes a Brahmin by birth, is manifestly false and erroneous.[*]

Now what can you reply to this ? Some of you will doubtless say, " Oh ! it doesn't matter about the mother. Even if one's mother does not happen to be a Brahmin

[*] See Appendix, pages 210, 211.

woman, it is quite enough that he have a Brahmin for his father. Whoever or whatever the mother may be, all the children of a Brahmin father are necessarily Brahmins." Now if this is true, it follows, that, when Brahmins have adulterous connection with harlots, the sons born to those harlots are necessarily Brahmins. But do you ever acknowledge such children to be Brahmins, and do you admit them to the privileges of your Brahminical caste? No, you do not. Hence your assertion, that "it matters nothing what the mother may be, so long as the father is a Brahmin," plainly will not answer your purpose.

Again, if you assert, that none but Brahmins' sons are Brahmins; a grave doubt at once arises as to who, among professed Brahmins now living, are really Brahmins, and who not. It is a fact well known to all, that the lawful wives of Brahmins not unfrequently play the harlot, and secretly commit adultery with Sudras. Hence it cannot certainly be known whether the sons, born to such erring Brahminee women, are the children of Brahmin fathers, or of Sudra fathers. How then are we to determine, who, among reputed Brahmins now living, are the sons of Sudras, and who the sons of Brahmins? All of them alike go about wearing the garb and the outward appearance of Brahmins. All equally claim and all equally receive the title of Brahmins.

SECOND.

THE FACT, THAT BRAHMINHOOD IS DESTROYED BY CERTAIN SPECIFIED ACTIONS, PROVES, THAT NO MAN IS A BRAHMIN BY VIRTUE MERELY OF HIS LINEAGE.

Hear what Tiruvalluvar says.

CURAL : 14TH CHAPTER : 4TH STANZA,

Literal Translation.

" A Brahmin, though he forget the Veda, may by study recover it; but let him fail in his caste duties, and his birth itself will be destroyed."

General Meaning.

A Brahmin, who has lost his Vedic learning, may recover it by reading ; but a Brahmin, who breaks the rules of his caste, thereby irreparably forfeits his very Brahminhood.

Observe also what is said in the Mahab'harat.

NALLA PILLAI B'HARATA : ANUSASANIKA PARUVAM : UMAMAKESVARA SAMVATA SARUKKAM.

Literal Translation.

"Oh lamp-like (Parvati) ! Those (Brahmins,) who indulge in anger, avarice, murder, sin, delusion, falsehood, lust, or pride, become Sudras."

General Meaning.

In this verse, Siva instructs Parvati thus ; "Oh lamp-like Parvati ! All Brahmins, who get angry ; all, who are avaricious ; all, who commit murder ; all, who are deluded ; all, who tell lies ; all, who indulge in lust or in pride, thereby lose their caste and become Sudras."

Furthermore ; the Manava Dharmma Sastra declares, that if a Brahmin sells meat, gum-lac, or salt ; his caste is at once forfeited thereby : and again, that if he sells milk for three days ; he becomes thereby a Sudra.*

What strange and marvellous teaching is this ? Let a horse, for instance, do whatever he may ; can he thereby cease to be a horse, and become of the pig species ? No. Being a horse by birth, it matters not how wicked or fractious he may be, he can never become a pig. Once a horse, he must always remain a horse. So, by parity of reasoning, if one is by birth a Brahmin ; let him do what he may, he cannot lose his caste and become a Sudra. Once a Brahmin, he must always remain a Brahmin. But here your Sastra positively declares, that if a Brahmin ventures to sell a little salt or a little milk, he forthwith changes into a Sudra. Whence it is certain, that mere birth makes no man a Brahmin.

* See Appendix, page 211.

But this is not all, for the stanza just quoted forces us to the further conclusion, that there are no Brahmins at all in existence. It positively affirms, that Brahmins who indulge in lust, or anger, or avarice, or pride, are not Brahmins, but Sudras. Tell us now, has any one, up to this time, ever seen a Brahmin, who was free from avarice and pride ?

THIRD.

YOUR RENOWNED SAGES HAVE TAUGHT, THAT, IN WHAT-EVER CASTE MEN MAY HAVE BEEN BORN, THE GOOD ONLY AMONG THEM ARE BRAHMINS, WHILE THE WICKED ARE ALL SUDRAS. THIS ALSO PROVES, THAT NO ONE IS A BRAHMIN BY VIRTUE MERELY OF HIS BIRTH.

KAPILA.

Literal Translation.

" Oh Fools ! can high birth confer any good, when dig-nity and morality are wanting ?"

General Meaning.

Not high birth, but honor and a just deportment are the proofs of good caste.

Kousika Muni is still more explicit.

NALLA PILLAI B'HARATA : ARAN'YA PARUVAM : KOUSIKA SARUKKAM.

Literal Translation.

" The great Rishis, conversant with the Vedas, have de-clared, that he only is a Brahmin, who has established for himself upon earth a reputation for truth, morality, and justice ; while he, who errs in these respects, is mani-festly a Sudra, even though he happen to be of Brahmin lineage. Is there any meaning then in the assertion, that one will be born a Brahmin after the death of his present body ? Oh faultless One ! Art not thou, (though only a wild huntsman,) thyself, in this birth, a guru of the Vedas ? Reflect and determine."

General Meaning.

A common huntsman having given most fitting answers to all the questions put to him by the great Muni Kousika, the Muni addressed him as follows. " Oh blameless One ! A man, be he of what caste he may, who conducts himself justly, honorably, and truthfully is a Brahmin. All whose behaviour is at variance with such good dispositions are Sudras, even though they may be Brahmins by lineage. So say the great Rishis, who have studied the Vedas. Hence it is absurd to say, that such and such persons will be Brahmins in a subsequent birth. Oh excellent Huntsman ! Goodness has made even you a Brahmin in this present birth."

Here Kousika tells us, that a man, who indulges in falsehood and deceit, though he may be of Brahmin descent, is not a Brahmin, but a Sudra : and that every man of good dispositions is, by virtue of his goodness, a Brahmin, even though he may by birth be a low huntsman. Whence it plainly appears, that if a Brahmin is destitute of good qualities, he thereby ceases to be a Brahmin ; and that if a Sudra is possessed of good qualities, he thereby becomes a Brahmin worthy of the name.*

Many others also of your celebrated sages and men eminent for learning bear the same testimony. Hear, for example, what Vemanar says.† " Call no good man a Chuckler, or a Pariah. Did not the great Muni, Vasisht'ha, marry a woman of the Chuckler caste ? How can a wicked man be called a Brahmin ? He is fit only to be pronounced a Pariah." This being so, it is evident that, in the estimation of your great men, high birth really counts for nothing. It cannot of itself make any man a Brahmin.

Furthermore, if it be true, as Kousika says, that a Brahmin who tells lies is no Brahmin ; then we must

---

* See Appendix, page 212.

† See Appendix, page 212.

conclude again, that there are really no Brahmins upon earth. For who ever saw a Brahmin, that did not tell lies ? None need be told how prevalent falsehood and deceit are among the members of that self-exalted caste.

FOURTH.

THE ABSENCE OF ALL PHYSICAL TRAITS, EVIDENCING BRAHMINS TO HAVE SPRUNG FROM THE FACE OF BRAHMA, PROVES THAT NO MAN IS A BRAHMIN BY VIRTUE MERELY OF HIS BIRTH,

We can discover no such traits, however diligently we search for them. It is impossible to distinguish many Brahmins as Brahmins merely from their appearance. If Washermen, Potters, and others should go about in Brahmin disguise, no one judging merely by sight could say, that they were not real Brahmins. Where then, we ask, are the peculiar traits which prove, that Brahmins sprung from the face of Brahma ? Is not their existence purely imaginary ? Pending the absence of all such distinguishing physical traits, we must be allowed to dissent from those who claim, that any one becomes a Brahmin, by virtue merely of his birth.

Oh Brahmins ! You regard all, who are not of yourselves, with sovereign contempt. You say to them, " We are a pure caste ; you are impure. Touch us not lest we be defiled. Come not near us, for your very presence is polluting." But why all this arrogance ? Is not your pride founded upon vanity and falsehood ? You talk largely of pollution ? By what standard is it to be measured ? Whence does it spring ? We ask you for reasons and explanations. Give them to us, if you can. The filth discharged from the " nine apertures" of the human body is, so far as we have ascertained, common to the entire race. As Vemanar well says,* filth and pollution belong equally to all without exception even at their birth. The same uncleanness, which is

* See Appendix, page 213.

found in other men by nature, is found also in you. Why then do you so arrogantly contemn, and vilify them as impure; and on what grounds do you so haughtily pronounce their very touch or approach a pollution?

Oh ye Brahmins! This arrogant claim of superiority above all other men not being sufficient to meet the demands of your exorbitant pride and swollen vanity, you have gone still further, and dared even to call yourselves gods,

NALLA PILLAI B'HARATA : SANTI PARUVAM ;
VIDUMANAI KANDA SARUKKAM.

Litteral Translation.

" Renown, power, ability to destroy enemies, the removal of guilt, the subjection of the five senses, all these are owing to Brahmins. Know, Oh far-famed One! that all the wealth and power of faultless monarchs are conferred upon them by the benedictions of Priests skilled in the Rig Veda."

General Meaning.

This verse declares, that Brahmins are gods of the earth, and that their blessing alone can confer upon kings renown, supremacy, power to overthrow enemies, extinction of guilt, mastery over the senses, and, in short, every description of regal wealth and prosperity.

Oh Brahmins! This verse perplexes and bewilders us beyond measure. If the ability of annihilating all enemies is really in your hands; how is it, that you have for so many years been subject first to the Mahommedans, and afterwards to the white man? If other men really derive all their power from you; how is it that so many among yourselves are afflicted with defects and deformities both physical and mental? If kings are really indebted to you for their self-mastery, and the expiation of their sins; how is it that not a few among yourselves commit crimes, and are, by the sentences of those very kings, consigned sometimes to fetters, and sometimes to the gallows? If you really confer upon others all the wealth and health they have; how are we to account for the facts, that many of you live by begging, and that not a few among you are afflicted with leprosy and other loathsome diseases? If you are really gods of the earth; how happens it, that such large numbers of your caste serve humbly in the Cutcheries of gentlemen? Answer us candidly; is not all this vaunting and glorification of yourselves the merest gasconade? Is it not the emptiest of boasting, as unequivocal and transparent as that of the swaggerer, whom one of your proverbs represents as saying, "Give me some old rice, and I will give you a medicine which prevents all hunger?" The truth is, your claims are simply ludicrous. There is no difference between you and other men.

Oh Brahmins! Renounce your absurd delusions, and clear your minds of their obscurity. Know that all men are of equal caste by nature, and that there is by birth no such thing as highness and lowness of caste.* Recognize the fact, that you equally with all other men are sinners, and that, unless your sins are removed, you equally with them will surely fall into hell. Cease your silly boastings then, and seek the true way of salvation, whereby you may secure the remission of your sins and gain heaven.

There is upon earth one only religion, which secures the removal of sin. Jesus Christ is the Author of that religion. He, and He alone, is the Lord of all worlds. He created you and all other men. For you and for all other men He became incarnate as a man upon Earth. He dwelt here thirty-three years. He revealed truth and instructed the people. Wherever He went, He healed sickness and disease. He cast out demons and devils. He gave life to the dead. Sinless, He took upon Himself the sins of the world. He, the Almighty, bore that heavy burden. To remove the sins of men, He endured great agonies. It was for this

* See Appendix, page 213.

that He died, nailed to the cross. On the third day, He rose again from the dead. Thus He expiated and removed the sins of all, who attach themselves to Him. He took upon Himself a penalty equivalent to the punishment of hell which was due to them. After dying, and rising again from the dead, He ascended up to heaven. There He now reigns the supreme Lord of the Universe. Whoever in this life renounces the ways of sin, believes in Jesus Christ, and walks according to His Word, him Jesus Christ saves from hell, and him Jesus Christ will bring to heaven, that he may remain there for ever with Himself in glory. All, on the other hand, who fail to accept Jesus Christ and believe in Him as their Saviour, will be turned into eternal hell.

Oh Brahmins! Listen kindly while we relate a pleasant story of a man of your own caste.

In the North country, there is a sacred place, which takes its name from the temple of Jaganāth. Multitudes of people from all parts of India make pilgrimages to this shrine. Some years ago, a Brahmin, named Gangātharan, was living in that place. This Brahmin, fully believing the image of Jaganāth, which is set up in the great temple there, to be truly god, worshipped it habitually. One day, however, he happened to buy a small book, which treated of Christianity. In it he read, that the image of Jaganāth is not god, and that all idolatry is vain and sinful. This at once excited him to anger. "What sort of talk is this," he exclaimed in a rage, "do they dare to say, that this image, which my forefathers and I have so long adored, is not a god?" But as he reflected more and more upon the arguments set forth in that little book, doubts began to arise in his mind. Again he read it, and again he pondered its contents. He also prayed, that God would reveal to him the truth. His doubts increased and gained strength from day to day. He was plunged in deepest sorrow, and felt unhappy as one, who, beaten about by the rough waves of the sea, is unable to descry the shore. Then he remembered the grace of the Lord Jesus Christ, and the sufferings He endured for sinners. Day after day he reflected upon the matter. "The image I worship," thought he within himself, "cannot remove my sins, nor do any good to my soul: Jesus Christ, the meritorious Guru, who loved me and gave His life for my life, is the truly gracious one." For some time, he was thus tossed from side to side, filled with anxiety and finding no relief. Finally he determined upon his course of action. Going out, he purchased the ramrod of a gun, and sharpened one end of it to a point. Carefully concealing his intentions, he waited till nightfall. Then, dreading lest he should be discovered, he crept secretly and silently into the vast temple, and, carefully picking his way into its innermost recesses, placed himself behind the image which squatted there. "Now," said he to himself, "I shall test the power of this idol: I must know whether it is a god, or a mere helpless block: I am determined to resolve the question, though I die for it. This doubt and this sorrow I am unable longer to carry." And with that he lifted the iron in the air. But just then a great fear took hold of him. "Believing this image of Jaganāth to be truly god," thought he, "my parents, relations and ancestors all worshipped it as such, and taught me also to do the same. If what they have told me is true, my life is not worth a moment's purchase, for this image will destroy me in the twinkling of an eye." Filled with apprehension, he stood transfixed, his heart palpitating with fear, his body quivering and bathed in a cold clammy sweat. "Come what will, my doubts must be solved, now or never" said he at last, and summoning up all his courage, he, with the energy of desperation, thrust the sharp point of the rod into Jaganāth. Jaganāth remained perfectly still. He neither moved, nor shrieked, nor so much as asked why he had been stabbed. Thereupon the Brahmin recovered from his terror and bewilderment. Running rapidly around, he struck and stabbed Jaganāth on every side, until thoroughly satisfied that he was a mere block and no god. Then issuing forth from the temple, he publicly avowed Jesus Christ as his God and Guru, and soon after joyfully embraced the Christian religion. Subsequently he preached the Christian Veda far and wide, and, by his faithful exhibition of its truths, caused large numbers of his countrymen to renounce heathenism, and become followers of Jesus the Saviour.

Oh Brahmins! May you all, like him, renouncing as chaff and rubbish your idolatry, your false religions, your vain caste observances, and your wicked pride, become hearty followers of the Lord Jesus Christ, the Saviour of the world!

APPENDIX to No. XIII.

ILLUSTRATIONS AND EXAMPLES.

(1.) The Brahmin is superior to all other men.

MENU 1 : 93.

Literal Translation.

" The Brahmin, because he sprung from the most eminent part, and because he was the first-born, and because he is possessed of the Vedas, is by right the lord of this whole creation."

General Meaning.

Since the Brahmin sprung from Brahma's face, was the first-born, and has possession of the Vedas, he is by right lord of the whole earth.

(2.) Examples showing, that Brahminhood is not derived from birth.

SANSCRIT SLOKA.

Literal Translation.

" The great Muni Visvāmitra, who was born from the womb of a low-caste woman, became a Brahmin by performing austerities ; hence birth was not the cause. The great Muni Nārada, who sprung from the womb of a Betel-creeper, became a Brahmin by performing austerities ; hence birth was not the cause. Although not the sons of Brahmin mothers, they are Brahmins to the world. Whoever has good qualities and is truthful is a Brahmin. Hence birth is not the cause. Correct deportment is the chief thing. Caste is not the chief thing. Of what use is caste without good manners ?"

General Meaning.

Visvāmitra, the son of a low-caste woman, and Nārada, the offspring of a Betel-creeper, both attained to the rank of Brahmins by the practice of religious austerities. Since these two great Munis became Brahmins, though neither of them had a Brahmin mother ; it is plain that mere caste or birth is not a ground of superiority. He, whose disposition and conduct are good, is the true Brahmin. Deportment, and not lineage, is the great criterion. Rank separated from virtue confers no pre-eminence.

(3.) Kapila and Tiruvalluvar were the sons of Pariah women.

KAPILAR AGAVAL.

Literal Translation.

" I am that Kapila, who was born to the great Muni and rigid ascetic Bhagavan, from the womb of the celebrated Pariah woman Ati, then a resident of the large city named Karuvūr. Tiruvalluvar grew up among the Pariahs, in Mailāpūr, a town of the Tonda country celebrated for the excellence of its Tamil."

General Meaning.

Kapila and Tiruvulluvar, both of them sons of a Pariah woman, were men of acknowledged eminence.

(4.) Brahminhood is destroyed by selling fish, salt, &c.

MENU 10 : 92.

" By selling flesh-meat, lacsha,* or salt, a Brahmin immediately falls low ; by selling milk three days, he becomes a Sudra."

* A species of gum-lac, from which a red color is extracted.

General Meaning.

A Brahmin loses his caste immediately by selling flesh, gum-lac, or salt. If he sells milk three days, he is thereby degraded to the rank of a Sudra.

(5.) True Brahminhood consists only in virtue.

B'HARATA,

Literal Translation.

" Even a Sudra, if his disposition and conduct are good, becomes a Brahmin ; while a Brahmin, if destitute of virtue, sinks lower even than a Sudra.

General Meaning.

A man of virtuous temper and deportment is a Brahmin, even though he be by birth a Sudra. A man devoid of virtue is lower than a Sudra, even though by birth he be a Brahmin.

(6.) The same as the foregoing.

B'HARATA,

Literal Translation.

" Oh Ud'hishdra ! No one becomes a Brahmin by lineage. No one becomes a Brahmin by caste. No one becomes a Brahmin by ceremonial rites. But a low-caste man may become a Brahmin, if he conducts himself virtuously."

General Meaning.

Neither lineage, nor caste, nor ceremonial rites can make a man a Brahmin; but virtue makes even a Pariah a Brahmin.

(7.) No man, who has a good disposition, ought to be called a Chuckler.*

VEMANAR 3 : 229.

Literal Translation.

" Oh Vemanar, beloved of the Lord ! If one has a virtuous disposition, we may not call him a Chuckler. Did not (the Brahmin) Vasisht'ha marry a Chuckler woman ?

---

* Chucklers are workers in leather. The word means a flesh-eater. They are reckoned one of the very lowest castes.

If a man is possessed of a Chuckler's disposition, can he be a Brahmin ?"

General Meaning.

Those only, who have virtuous dispositions, are of high caste.

(8.) At birth, all men are equal in caste.

VEMANAR 3: 225.

Literal Translation.

" Oh Vemanar, beloved of the Lord! Let us have no contentions about high and low castes. All castes are equal at birth. How can we distinguish the high from the low ?"

General Meaning.

There is no need of discussing about caste distinctions. At birth, men of all castes are on a common level. How then can we distinguish this one as high, and that one as low ?

(9.) At birth, filth and pollution belong to all indiscriminately.

VEMANAR 3: 111.

Literal Translation.

" Oh Vemanar! Pollution! Pollution! Touch us not, they cry. But where (we ask) does this pollution begin, and where does it end? The pollution, arising from the filth contained in the nine apertures, is born with all men, at the time of their birth."

General Meaning.

" Touch us not," they cry out, " Touch us not, lest we be polluted." But whence this pollution ? What its origin ? What its termination ? The filth, which oozes from the nine apertures of the human body is what really pollutes one, and this filth is common to all men, for it is born with them.

(10.) Brahminhood is not conferred by Sastras, religious rites, &c.

SANSCRIT SLOKA.

Literal Translation.

" Therefore Brahminhood is not conferred by the Sastra, nor by ceremonial rites, nor by birth, nor by lineage, nor by the Veda, nor by actions."

General Meaning.

The Sastra, ceremonies, birth, lineage, the veda, actions; none of all these can make a man a Brahmin.

APPENDIX. No. XIV.

VARIOUS TOPICS.

STREET OPPONENTS, UNFAIR DISPUTANTS, AND CAVILLERS.

FIRST.

THE PROFITLESS DISPUTANT.

CURAL 20, 10.

Literal Translation.

" Among words, speak such as are useful. Among words, speak not such as are useless."

General Meaning.

When engaged in discussion, be careful to omit all unmeaning or superfluous words, and to employ only such as are fitting and necessary.

SECOND.

THE BOASTFUL DISPUTANT.

Self-conceit is a proof of ignorance.

CURAL 85, 4.

Literal Translation.

" Would you know what ignorance is ? It is that pride, which says, ' We are the possessors of knowledge.' "

General Meaning.

An ostentatious parade of knowledge or of learning has in it the very essence of ignorance.

Great men deport themselves humbly : Base men praise themselves.

CURAL 98, 8.

Literal Translation.

"The great man is always humble; the small man admires and vaunts himself."

General Meaning.

The truly great are always distinguished for their modesty; while insignificant men are known by their ostentatious swaggering.

THIRD.
THE ANGRY DISPUTANT.
1st.—ANGER IS INJURIOUS.

It is a foe to happiness.

CURAL 31, 4.

Literal Translation.

"Is there any enemy greater than anger, which kills both laughter and joy?"

General Meaning.

There is no greater enemy than anger.

———

It destroys its subjects.

CURAL 31, 5.

Literal Translation.

"If a man wishes to guard himself (against the approach of evil,) let him guard against (the approach of) anger: if he does not do so, anger will kill him."

General Meaning.

Indulge not anger, lest it prove your destroyer.

———

It injures the disposition, and ruins the soul.

VEMANAR 3, 60.

Literal Translation.

"Oh Vemanar, Beloved of the Lord! The pit of hell is reached by anger. The temper is marred by anger. Life is shortened by anger."

General Meaning.

Anger debases a man's disposition, shortens his life, and finally plunges him into perdition.

2nd.—ADMONITIONS AGAINST INDULGING ANGER.

The reproof of a friend is better than the flattery of an enemy.

NALADIAR 8, 3.

Literal Translation.

" Provided your counsellors are wise men, be assured, Oh King ! that the harsh words of loving friends are better than the honeyed expressions of flattering enemies."

General Meaning.

The harsh but faithful words of a true friend are less injurious than the sweet but deceitful flatteries of a secret foe.

Avoid anger, for it is the cause of many evils.

CURAL 31, 3.

Literal Translation.

" Forget anger towards every one ; for by it is occasioned the birth of all evils."

General Meaning.

Refrain from anger, for it is the fruitful source of evils innumerable.

Carefully govern your tongue.

CURAL 13, 7.

Literal Translation.

" Though men guard nothing else, let them guard their tongues ; for if they do not, they will be drawn into faulty expressions, and will suffer distress."

General Meaning.

Though you govern nothing else, govern at least your tongue.

Get not angry; but hear attentively, and consider.

VEMANAR 1, 143.

Literal Translation.

" Oh Vemanar ! Whoever the speaker, we should listen to him. While listening, we should be dispassionate and consider. He, who listens, ponders, and masters what he hears, is a just man."

General Meaning.

Whoever may be the speaker, we should give him a hearing. Having listened calmly and dispassionately, we should ponder well what has been said. He, who thus listens, ponders, and understands, is sure to arrive at just conclusions.

FOURTH.

THE NOISY DISPUTANT.

VEMANAR 1, 30.

Literal Translation.

" Oh Vemanar, Beloved of the Lord ! A mean person always speaks ostentatiously. A good man speaks gently. Will gold clang as bell-metal does ?"

General Meaning.

Insignificant persons are evermore clamorous; but the tone of a wise man is always gentle. Gold never clangs like bell-metal.

A dry palm-leaf rattles; a green one is noiseless.

NALADIAR 26, 6.

Literal Translation.

" No sound comes from the green leaves of the palmyra tree, but its dry leaves rustle noisily evermore. So learned and wise men, fearing lest they be betrayed into faulty expressions, keep silence ; but ignorant men are always jabbering."

General Meaning.

The wise are sparing of their words; but the ignorant are for ever gabbling.

FIFTH.

THE ABUSIVE DISPUTANT.

Abusers are always contemptible persons.

NALADIAR 33, 1.

Literal Translation.

" Senseless as a ladle, which knows not the sweetness of the gruel, empty-headed fools ridicule the words of loving men, who discourse graciously on virtue. The wise however accept those words as full of substance.

General Meaning.

Fools scornfully ridicule the discourses of gracious men; but the learned accept them as excellent.

———

Abuse scorches the Abuser.

NALADIAR 7, 3.

Literal Translation.

" Words spoken by an unguarded tongue always scorch the speakers themselves. Hence, men of mature wisdom and intelligence will never hastily give utterance to harsh and angry expressions."

General Meaning.

Harsh and abusive language scorches its utterer. Therefore wise men never allow themselves to be betrayed into its use.

———

The great are grieved at the punishment, which overtakes abusers.

NALADIAR 6, 8.

Literal Translation.

" It is the duty of great men not only to forgive abuse cast upon themselves; but also to grieve, because their vilifiers must, as a consequence of their wicked conduct, fall into a fiery hell."

General Meaning.

Truly great men not only suffer abuse patiently ; but are also saddened by the thought, that their abusers must, as the result of their misconduct, fall into the flames of hell.

SIXTH.

THE OBSCENE DISPUTANT.

Great men grieve at the disgrace, which an obscene person brings upon his mother.

NALADIAR 32, 6.

Literal Translation.

" When fools, who have failed to profit by instruction, speak detestable words ; wise and excellent men feel ashamed, and greatly pity the mother, who gave birth to those fools."

General Meaning.

When ignorant fools utter obscene language ; wise men are deeply distressed at thought of the obloquy such persons bring upon the mothers who bore them.

SEVENTH.

THE DISPUTANT, WHO SCORNS AND REJECTS TRUTH.

NALADIAR 26, 9.

Literal Translation.

" Base and contemptible souls are like the fly, which, passing by the honey distilled in perfume-breathing flowers, greedily seeks everything that is foul and disgusting. Of what profit to such persons are the clear and sweet words, which drop, nectar-like, from the lips of the great and the wise ?"

General Meaning.

Base and contemptible souls refuse to profit by the instructions of wise and excellent men.

ON BECOMING A CHRISTIAN.

People make various objections to embracing Christianity. We notice here a few of the more common ones.

FIRST.

HOW CAN I BECOME A CHRISTIAN? IT IS AN EXTREMELY DIFFICULT THING.

CURAL 3, 6.

Literal Translation.

" The great will do those things, which are hard to do : the mean cannot do those things, which are hard to do."

General Meaning.

The great will do what duty requires, however difficult may be the task; but mean men shrink irresolute, and leave it undone.

SECOND.

HOW CAN I EMBRACE CHRISTIANITY, WHEN BY SO DOING I MUST SUFFER GREAT PERSECUTION?

Do that which in the end confers happiness.

CURAL 67, 9.

Literal Translation.

" Though much trouble arise at the outset, let men resolutely do those things, which in the end result in happiness."

General Meaning.

Present inconvenience should never be made an excuse for not doing that, which will in the end confer true happiness.

———

Do not men undergo great troubles in order to obtain earthly good ?

NITINERI VILAKKAM, 53.

Literal Translation.

" Those, whose occupation is to them like their eyes, pay no regard to physical suffering : They know no hunger :

They seek no sleep : They fear no injury that others may do them : They deem no time unseasonable : They dread no dishonor."

General Meaning.

Men resolutely bent on the accomplishment of an object disregard bodily suffering and all other inconveniences.

THIRD.

How am I to live, if I become a Christian ?

Vemanar 2, 95.

Literal Translation.

" Why, Oh Soul ! dost thou fret about the stomach ? The stomach will be satisfied some how or other. Has not even the frog, which lives in stone, a stomach ?"

General Meaning.

Worry not about the stomach, Oh my Soul ! for in some way or other it is sure to be replenished. Even a frog imbedded in stone has a stomach.

FOURTH.

What shall I gain by embracing Christianity ?

Kathamanjari, 53rd Story.

A Stork sitting on the edge of a tank saw an approaching Swan, whereupon the following dialogue took place.

Stork. " How exquisitely tinted your legs and beak and eyes are ! Who are you, and from whence do you come ?"

Swan. " I am a Swan, and I come from the world of the gods."

Stork. " Tell me, I pray you, in what part of that world you reside, and what sort of a place it is ?"

Swan. " I live on a magnificent lake called Mānasa. Its water is exceedingly sweet and limpid. Its banks, composed of precious stones, are adorned with celestial trees and golden hued lotus flowers."

STORK. " How beautiful ! And is it well stocked with snails ?"

SWAN. " No, there are no snails in it at all."

STORK. " Pish! Begone ! Of what use is a lake whose waters contain no snails ?"

MORAL.

In like manner, foolish men, who lust after earthly pleasures, shun the path, which leads to celestial joys.

ON EATING MEAT.

FIRST.

IT IS LAWFUL TO EAT MEAT.

MENU 5, 30.

Literal Translation.

" Though one eat daily the flesh of animals, which may lawfully be eaten, he does not thereby become a sinner. Were not both animals, which may be eaten, and men, who eat them, equally created by Brahma ?"

General Meaning.

Since both animals fit for food, and men who eat them were equally created by Brahma; it follows, that those, who eat the flesh of such animals, incur no guilt, even though they partake of it day after day.

SECOND.

ANIMALS MAY BE KILLED FOR SACRIFICE AND FOR FOOD. AGASTYA HIMSELF KILLED THEM FOR THESE PURPOSES.

MENU 5, 22.

Literal Translation.

" Beasts and birds of excellent kinds may be killed by Brahmins for sacrifice, and for the sustenance of their dependants. Did not Agastya do this of old ?"

General Meaning.

Beasts and birds may be slain for sacrifice and for food, since the great Muni Agastya did this of old.

THIRD.

THOSE, WHO DECLARE IT UNLAWFUL TO KILL AND
EAT LIVING THINGS, SHOULD, ACCORDING TO THEIR
OWN DOCTRINE, ABSTAIN FROM EATING ANYTHING
WHATSOEVER.

Fruits, vegetables and the like are " living things
possessed of a single sense ;" therefore they ought not
to eat them.

Neither may they eat dried leaves, &c., for that
would be all the same as if they should eat dead bodies,
from which the life has departed.

Since water teems with life, they must altogether
abstain from that also.

Hence it is clear, that those who teach this doctrine
should, in consistency, neither eat nor drink anything
whatsoever. In fact, they are themselves bound by
their teaching to die as soon as possible from hunger
and thirst.

The authors of this doctrine were evidently ignorant
of the fact, that water is full of living creatures. Else
they would never have promulgated their indiscrimi-
nate laws against the destruction of life. But the true
God, who placed those living creatures in water, has
in His Holy Word granted men permission to slay
such animals as are fitted and necessary for their food.

WE CANNOT LIVE WITHOUT LYING
AND CHEATING.

FIRST.

LIARS ARE LIKE CRACKED EARTHEN VESSELS.
VEMANAR 1, 70.

Literal Translation.

" Hear Oh Vemanar, Beloved of the Lord ! How can
prosperity dwell in the houses of those, who tell many lies ?
It must pass away like water poured into a broken vessel."

General Meaning.

Prosperity will no more abide in the houses of liars, than water will abide in a cracked earthen vessel.

SECOND.

STOLEN WEALTH IS SURE TO PERISH.

CURAL 29, 3.

Literal Translation.

" Wealth acquired by fraud will pass its bounds and perish, even while it seems to increase."

General Meaning.

Property got by cheating may seem for a time to increase ; but in the end it is sure to perish.

THIRD.

HONESTY IS PROFITABLE.

CURAL 12, 10.

Literal Translation.

" To protect the property of others as carefully as they do their own, is to merchants the best of merchandize.

General Meaning.

Guarding the property of others as carefully and as honestly, as if it were one's own, is the noblest type of merchandize.

AFFLICTIONS OF THE RIGHTEOUS.

VEMANAR 2, 72.

Literal Translation.

" Hear, Oh Vemanar, Beloved of the Lord ! The Washerman, after beating clothes and removing their dirt, folds them up neatly. If (in like manner) a good counsellor beat us, what then ? (Shall we complain ?)"

General Meaning.

A Washerman beats soiled clothes to remove their stains. Those being removed, he folds them up care-

fully and neatly.   Shall we then murmur, when a sure
friend pains us by giving us good advice ?

FOUR YUGAS.

THEIR LENGTH STATED IN YEARS.

1st. The Satya or Kirēta Yuga equals (1,728,000)
one million, seven hundred and twenty-eight thousand
years.

2nd. The Tirēta Yuga equals (1,296,000) one million, two hundred and ninety-six thousand years.

3rd. The Tuvāpara Yuga equals (864,000) eight
hundred and sixty-four thousand years.

4th. The Kali Yuga equals (432,000) four hundred
and thirty-two thousand years.

WE ARE TOLD THAT THE SATYA YUGA WAS A SINLESS
AGE, AND THAT THE "INSTITUTES OF MENU" WERE
WRITTEN WITHIN THAT PERIOD.

SANSCRIT SLOKA.

Literal Translation.

" The Dharmma Sastra was made by me, Menu, at the
command of Brahma, in the month Avani, after one
hundred thousand years of the truth-abounding Satya
Yuga had elapsed."

General Meaning.

The Mānava Dharmma Sastra was written in the
sinless Satya Yuga.

THE MANAVA DHARMMA SASTRA ITSELF BEARS WITNESS,
THAT THE AGE IN WHICH MENU LIVED WAS MORE
SINFUL THAN THE KALI YUGA.

MENU 2, 215.

Literal Translation.

" Let no man sit in solitary places with his mother, or
his sister, or his daughter. The powerful assemblage of
corporeal organs will drag even wise men (into sin.)"

General Meaning.

Lust is strong enough to drag even the wisest men into sin. Therefore let no man venture to remain alone with his own mother, sister, or daughter.

From the above quotations, we are convinced not only that sin prevailed during the Satya Yuga; but also that the existence itself of the four Yugas is a myth.

Furthermore the Hindu Sastras relate that, during the progress of this same Satya Yuga celebrated for its freedom from sin, the gods and the Asuras fought with each other when engaged in churning the sea of milk; that Brahma sought to ravish his own daughter, and that Siva lusted after Vishnu, when the latter had assumed a female form.

MARRIAGE.

FIRST.

THE DOMESTIC STATE IS MORE HONORABLE THAN THE ASCETIC STATE.

CURAL 5, 6.

Literal Translation.

" If a man lives virtuously in the Domestic State, what can he gain by going into the other ?"

General Meaning.

The man, who lives virtuously in the Domestic State, can gain nothing by entering into the Ascetic.

CURAL 5, 7.

Literal Translation.

" Among all those, who labor (to be emancipated from the bondage of sense,) he is the greatest who lives according to rule in the Domestic State."

General Meaning.

He, who lives in the Domestic State practising its virtues, is greater than all Ascetics.

SECOND.

A WIFELESS HOUSE IS A DESERT.

NALADIAR 37, 1.

Literal Translation.

" Of what use to a man, destitute of an excellent and virtuous wife, is his house, even though it be a cloud-reaching palace, magnificently furnished and filled with sparkling jewels ? It is like an unsightly desert, painful to be looked upon."

General Meaning.

Let a man's house be ever so magnificent, it is still only a desert, if he have not a good wife.

PROPERTY USELESS TO A MAN WITHOUT A WIFE.

VERRI VERKAI.

Literal Translation.

" Though a man possess the wealth of earth and heaven united ; he has nothing, if he have not a wife."

General Meaning.

Wealth, however great it be, is useless to the unmarried.

DRUNKENNESS.

FIRST.

THE TESTIMONY OF TIRUVALLUVAR.

THE DRUNKARD BECOMES LOATHSOME EVEN TO HIS OWN MOTHER.

CURAL 93, 3.

Literal Translation.

" Drunkenness is disgraceful even when indulged in only before one's mother. What then must it be, when practised in the presence of great men ?"

General Meaning.

Drunkenness is under all circumstances loathsome and disgraceful.

DRUNKENNESS BRINGS SHAME.
CURAL 93, 7.
Literal Translation.

" Those, who secretly drink toddy and get inebriated, will be spied out and laughed at by their neighbours."

General Meaning.

Drunkards are sure to be discovered and ridiculed by others.

THE REFORMATION OF DRUNKARDS IMPOSSIBLE.
CURAL 93, 9.
Literal Translation.

" Reasoning with a drunkard is like going under water with a torch in search of a drowned man."

General Meaning.

It is impossible to bring a drunkard to his reason.

AN EXHORTATION TO DRUNKARDS.
CURAL 93, 10.
Literal Translation.

" When a drunkard sees drunken men in his intervals of sobriety, he does not seem to think of his own degeneracy."

General Meaning.

If a drunkard, who in his sober hours sees others lying drunk, could only realize, that when himself drunk he is like those whom he sees, he would drink no more.

SECOND.
A PROVERB CONCERNING DRUNKENNESS.
Literal Translation.

" A drunkard's nature is the nature of a crow, a stork, a parrot, and a monkey."

General Meaning.

A Drunkard resembles the crow, the stork, the parrot, and the monkey.

The Crow not only eats carcasses itself; but gets other crows to come and eat with it.

The Stork, when watching for fish, assumes the appearance of a post; but, the moment opportunity offers, it seizes and devours them.

The Parrot repeats meaningless words incessantly.

The Monkey, never still, wanders about everywhere without an object.

Just so the Drunkard.   Not satisfied with drinking himself, he induces others to drink with him.   He tries to make men believe, that he does not drink ; yet drinks whenever opportunity offers.   His chattering and muttering are incessant and meaningless.   He wanders about objectless here, there, and everywhere.

THIRD.
THE EVILS OF DRUNKENNESS.

(1.)   IT BEWILDERS THE MIND.

(2.)   IT SQUANDERS PROPERTY.

(3.)   IT RUINS REPUTATION.

(4.)   IT UPSETS FAMILIES.

(5.)   IT KILLS THE BODY.

(6.)   IT DESTROYS THE SOUL.

So fearfully destructive is drunkenness both in this world and the next.

EXHORTATIONS.
FIRST.

REGARD NOT EARTHLY TREASURES AS TRUE WEALTH.

NALADIAR 28, 10.

Literal Translation.

" Acquiring wealth is a trouble.   Guarding abundant wealth acquired is, in like manner, a great trouble.   If the wealth thus guarded diminishes, that also is a trouble.   If it perishes, it is no less a trouble.   Hence wealth is the very dwelling-place of trouble."

General Meaning.

Wealth is evermore a source of trouble.

SECOND.

BEWARE LEST YOU BE DESTROYED.
NITINERI VILAKKAM 34.

Literal Translation.

" Though closely surrounded with fire, the Rock Snake moves not ; but sleeps on, heaving deep sighs. So ever is it with base persons. They perceive not destruction, though it approach them visibly."

General Meaning.

Indifference to threatening destruction is characteristic of the base.

THIRD.

FEAR THOSE THINGS, WHICH OUGHT TO BE FEARED.
CURAL 43, 8.

Literal Translation.

" It is folly not to fear what ought to be feared. To fear what ought to be feared is the part of wise men."

General Meaning.

Wise men fear those things, which ought to be feared.

FOURTH.

DO NOT PROCRASTINATE.
CURAL 54, 5.

Literal Translation.

" He, who has forgotten to guard beforehand against coming calamity, will, after the calamity comes, grieve over his carelessness."

General Meaning.

Whoever carelessly neglects providing against impending calamities will, after those calamities fall upon him, realize and mourn over his folly.

NALADIAR 34, 2.

Literal Translation.

" Those who say, ' It will be time enough to practise virtue after we have discharged the duties belonging to the Domestic State,' are like persons, who going down to the great Ocean to bathe, wait upon the shore, saying, ' We will bathe when its sounding shall have entirely subsided.' "

General Meaning.

Begin the practice of virtue without delay.

SUPERSTITIONS.
FIRST.

ASTROLOGY FALSE.

VEMANAR 3, 85.

Literal Translation.

" Hear, Oh Vemanar, Beloved of the Lord! Let those, who have thoroughly investigated the science of Astrology, tell how much it has accomplished. Reflection convinces us, that one's future is known only to God."

General Meaning.

The study of Astrology, however extensive it may be, is profitless. Our future is known to none but God.

Illustrations.

(1.) An Astrologer informed a King, that his Majesty's life would terminate in two years, while his own would be prolonged to twenty. No sooner were the words spoken, than the King's Prime Minister drew his sword, and decapitated the Astrologer.

(2.) An Astrologer, after announcing to a king, that his queen would give birth to a son, went secretly to the queen, and told her, that her child would be a daughter. A daughter was born. To the angry enquiries of the king, the Astrologer replied, " Fearing to tell your Majesty the truth, I confided it secretly to the queen. Ask her, and see if it be not so." Thus Astrologers deceive and gull their victims.

SECOND.

DIVINATION IS FOLLY.

KATHAMANJARI, 74TH STORY.

A certain man was told, that if the first thing he saw, on rising in the morning, was a pair of crows he would be particularly fortunate on that day. Summoning a servant he said, " Awake me to-morrow the moment you see a pair of crows." On the following day, the obedient servant, watching diligently until he saw two crows together, hastily awaked his master. Before the latter could rise and get out of doors however, one of the crows flew away, leaving its mate solitary and alone. Thereupon flying into a rage, the master cuffed and kicked his servant, saying, " Why, Villain ! did you not wake me before the other crow flew away ?" To this the servant replied, " Oh Sir ! Do you not perceive the fortune, which has befallen me, who saw both the crows ?" Hearing that, the master retired abashed.

WHY DO CHRISTIANS ATTEMPT IMPOSSIBILITIES ?

THE GREAT WILL TRY TO ACCOMPLISH A GOOD WORK, EVEN THOUGH IT SEEM AN IMPOSSIBILITY.

NITINERI VILAKKAM 49.

Literal Translation.

" Administering life-giving medicine to the dying is not a fault. If you ask why ; apparent impossibilities sometimes prove to be possibilities. Hence great men persevere to the end, even when the good they aim at seems unattainable."

General Meaning.

Great men labor on bravely and persistently in spite of the most discouraging circumstances.